© Disney

Disneyland®
Resort Paris

by Lindsay Hunt

Lindsay Hunt turned to travel journalism after
a career in publishing and a year sampling
tapas in Spain. She has researched many
destinations for *Holiday Which?*
magazine, and is co-author of several hotel
guides and a book on Spain.

Above: *Fantasyland, Disneyland® Park*

AA Publishing

*Adventureland,
Disneyland® Park*

Written by Lindsay Hunt
Revised by Apostrophe S Limited

© Automobile Association Developments Limited 1993,
1995, 2000, 2002, 2005
Maps © Automobile Association Developments Limited
2004
Reprinted Dec 2004

Published by AA Publishing, a trading name of Automobile
Association Developments Limited, whose registered
office is Southwood East, Apollo Rise, Farnborough,
Hampshire GU14 OJW. Registered number 1878835.

Automobile Association Developments Limited retains the
copyright in the original edition © 1993 and in all
subsequent editions, reprints and amendments.

A CIP catalogue record for this book is available from the
British Library.

A02483

Find out more about
AA Publishing and the
wide range of travel
publications and services
the AA provides by
visiting our website at
www.theAA.com/bookshop

Colour separation: Keenes, Andover
Printed and bound in Italy by Printer Trento S.r.l.

Contents

About this Book

This book is divided into four sections to cover the most important aspects of your visit to Disneyland® Resort Paris and the surrounding area.

Viewing *Disneyland* ® *Resort Paris*

pages 5–26

An introduction to the Resort by the author.

The Shaping of Disneyland® Resort Paris
The Facts & Figures
The Famous
The Background
The Features
The Essentials

What to See pages 27–82

The two parks of Disneyland® Resort Paris, each with its own brief introduction and an alphabetical listing of the main attractions. Plus a section on excursions, including Paris.

'Tip' boxes giving useful suggestions
Features
Practical information
Maps

Where To... pages 84–112

Detailed listings of the best places to eat, stay, shop and be entertained.

Practical Matters pages 114–124

A highly visual section containing essential travel information. These include health and safety, currency information, transport, details on opening times, charges and tickets. Finally there are useful words and phrases on the language page.

Prices

Where appropriate, an indication of the cost of an establishment is given by £ signs: £££ denotes higher prices, ££ denotes average prices, while £ denotes lower charges.

All prices quoted in this book were current at the time of going to press. However, as they are intended to serve as guidelines only, readers are storngly advised to check details with Disneyland Paris at the time of their visit.

Star Ratings

In this book attractions in the Disneyland® Resort Paris Parks are given ratings – from one to three stars. Every attraction is someone's favourite, and someone else's least favourite. You will not know if you like something unless you try it, so try not to prejudge anything. Have a go!

✪✪✪   Do not miss

✪✪   Highly recommended

✪   Worth seeing if you have time

© Disney

Viewing Disneyland® Resort Paris

Above: *Sleeping Beauty's Castle,
Disneyland® Park*

Shaping of Disneyland® Resort Paris

The idea of a Disney Park in Europe goes back nearly 20 years, though it was not until 1984 that The Walt Disney Company began to explore the possibilities seriously. The options were wide open. Would English-speaking Britain, whose citizens so eagerly patronise American Theme Parks, naturally play host to Mickey Mouse? Or should the new Disney Park be blessed with that cocktail of sunshine and oranges so successful in California and Florida – by being located in southern Spain, perhaps? Why not target the wealthy Germans? No doubt they could run the show as efficiently as Walt would have wished. Feasibility studies spawned; Team Disney anguished, and then began some hard bargaining. Eventually, the keys to the kingdom fell into French hands. The promised land was a stretch of unprepossessing sugar-beet fields about 20 miles (32km) east of Paris. Not immediately enticing, but the Marne-la-Vallée area had a number of advantages. For one thing, it was available. And there are not that many suitably sized tracts of affordable land available in Western Europe these days. Secondly, it lay slap in the middle of a cat's cradle of important communication networks linking the richest and most densely populated countries of Europe. And thirdly, it was on the eastern outskirts of the greater Paris area. It was, admittedly, a bit damper and chillier than one might have hoped, but you can't have everything.

Once Upon a Time

The Walt Disney Company signed a 30-year contract to develop the site with the French authorities in 1987. The French government purchased some 4,800 acres (1,940ha) of land, a total area about one-fifth the size of Paris, agreeing to release it to Disney as it was needed. Meanwhile, residents and farmers, now tenants instead of landlords, carried on their lives as normally as they could in a region destined for rapid and irrevocable change. Earth-moving and construction equipment arrived to shift millions of tons of topsoil into new configurations of lakes, railway tracks, road systems and protective circular ramparts, like some Iron Age hill-fort. The statistics were awesome, and the speed at which the project took shape was astonishing. Within four years Phase I of the development had been completed, covering 1,483 acres (600ha) of land. The region was transformed, with 450,000 trees and shrubs, several artificial expanses of water, and almost 20 miles (32km) of roads. Six extraordinary hotels and a 'trapper village' emerged from the fields, but more curious structures could be glimpsed behind the stockade

Whatever the Weather

When Disneyland® Park was first planned, there was some debate over Disney's prudence in placing it in Northern France instead of somewhere near the Mediterranean. There is no doubt that climate plays a significant role and the facts are incontrovertible: the resort looks truly magical in the sun, when its colours sparkle and the castle glitters. But there are advantages of going on a day when the weather is poor – the Theme Parks are less crowded and you will see far more attractions. Disney considered the weather, and have made a number of modifications to the design of the Parks to suit Northern France's climate. All visitor areas have central heating and air conditioning, and in many places, particularly hotels, shops and restaurants, you will find log fires roaring. More of the attractions and queuing areas are covered over than in America's Disney Parks, and most hotel swimming pools are covered. Large eaves also extend over queuing areas to protect waiting crowds at the attractions.

Left: *a firework display high above the Sleeping Beauty Castle*

European Influence
Throughout Walt's career he was a regular visitor to Europe and his work was greatly influenced by Europe's legends and fables. Fourteen of his animated films were inspired by famous European authors such as the Brothers Grimm (*Snow White and the Seven Dwarfs*), James M Barrie (*Peter Pan*), Rudyard Kipling (*The Jungle Book*), and many more.

Eurostar - a fast and efficient way to travel to Paris

surrounding the new Disney Park – a storybook castle, a piece of re-created Arizona, and a skull-like cave.

Against the Odds

Meanwhile, around the edges of the complex, speculation buzzed, both of the cerebral and mercenary kinds. Rumours of Disney's sinister transatlantic masterplan to undermine 'French Culture As We Know It Today' were fuelled, and many a pundit had a scornful crack at Mickey Mouse.

Not everyone liked the idea of a Disney Park on their doorstep. And, of course, some of the locals had to play the role of dispossessed serfs carefully, to maximise any potential return on their lost land. A crocodile tear or two would not be inappropriate in the circumstances. This controversial climate did not stop entrepreneurs from constructing motels and petrol stations in many of the surrounding villages. These extraneous developments, simply cashing in on the Disney bandwagon, have done

most to disrupt the area. Sadly, they are an inevitable consequence of such a huge investment, readily predictable from all the experiences of American Theme Parks.

Other unintentional effects of Disney's impact on this part of France are less tangible, but still worrying. A glance at local tourist literature produces the disconcerting sensation that the whole of the Seine-et-Marne region is turning into a sort of giant Theme Park. Many local authorities, spurred to commercial enterprise by Disney's example, are now promoting their tourist portfolios strongly as rival (or rather, supplementary) attractions. Every little sight and mildly pretty village is now paraded before the eyes of Disney patrons like some contestant in a game show. Summer pageants, medieval banquets and candlelit tours abound. With all this going on, there is a strong possibility that some visitors at least, dazed by the razzmatazz, will come to regard the great châteaux of the Île-de-France as mere clones of the Sleeping Beauty Castle.

Grand Design

The scale and scope of Disneyland® Resort Paris is by any standards a modern miracle, second in Europe only to the Channel Tunnel in terms of cost and engineering resources. The Sun King himself, Louis XIV, would have appreciated such an ambitious project.

Happy Ever After

For those who recognise the difference, however, the historic and cultural riches of the surroundings (including Paris, of course) must be regarded as one of Disneyland® Resort Paris's most appealing features. In the US, at Orlando and Anaheim, there are certainly dozens of things to do, but they are an oddly monochromatic mix of Theme Parks and contrived recreation. In France the texture of the holiday tapestry is infinitely more interesting and complex.

Controversy has now died down as the positive influence of the Disney Theme Parks on the area's economy is hard to deny. The creation of over 10,000 new jobs and 30,000 in the Île-de-France

© Disney

DISNEYLAND.
RESORT
PARIS

© Disney

region, as well as spin-offs for hoteliers and other local businesses, has been most welcome. The infrastructure of the area (road and rail connections, hotel accommodation, and so on) has been boosted out of all recognition. The region was now ready to welcome the new Walt Disney Studios® Park, which opened its gates a few days before the tenth anniversary of Disneyland® Resort Paris. The idea of a second European Disney park on the theme of cinema, animation and television goes back to 1992, just before Disneyland® Park opened, but Disney Imagineers were only given the green light to begin planning and designing the new park in 1997. They based their work on the concept of the successful Disney-MGM Studios at Walt Disney World in Florida and adapted their new creation to European audiences with the help of European professionals in the world of cinema, such as Rémy Julienne, the French stunt designer.

Some agonise, justifiably enough, over the un-Frenchness of it all. There are nods and winks at European fairy stories and children's classics, but basically Disneyland® Resort Paris is a heartily transatlantic product, as American as a prime rib steak. French culture, however, is nothing if not robust. The things many people love about France and the French way of life will survive the arrival of Mickey Mouse perfectly well. In any case, before we complain too loudly about the invasion of an alien culture, maybe there are some things about the land of Mickey Mouse that we Europeans should take note of: what, after all, is wrong with clean toilets, courteous staff, efficient transport systems and litter-free grounds? For the resort to be a success, all Disney needed was for enough people to turn up and enjoy themselves, and then tell their friends. This goal was easily reached, for enjoying yourself at Disneyland® Resort Paris is almost unavoidable. Where else can grown-up people ride on an elephant roundabout, or wear mouse ears, without feeling like idiots?

© Disney

Disney is what children's dreams are made of

Disneyland® Resort Paris in Figures

- Disneyland® Resort Paris property covers one fifth the size of Paris – 4,801 acres (1,943ha)
- 2,223 acres (900ha) have been developed to date
- There have been over 110 million visitors since the opening in 1992
- In 2002 there were 13.1 million visitors to the resort
- The average length of a stay is 3 nights, 4 days
- Over 1,000 artists work at the resort including actors, dancers, musicians and designers
- Disneyland® Park has more than 50 rides, shows and attractions
- More than 26 million items are sold every year in 42 shops and 23 stands
- The Sleeping Beauty Castle is 141ft (43m) high
- Space Mountain rockets reach a speed of 70km per hour and one rocket is launched every 36 seconds
- Catastrophe Canyon in Walt Disney Studios® Park uses 265,000 litres of water for each display and the water is recycled for each show
- There are 580,000 bricks on Main Street, U.S.A., laid out in a pattern similar to New York at the turn of the century
- There are 68 food and beverage locations at Disneyland® Resort Paris
- Up to 150,000 meals are served daily during peak periods
- 4 million hamburgers are eaten each year, 20 tonnes of fish and seafood and 700 tonnes of chicken
- 283 million tonnes of chips are consumed each year
- 6 million litres of Coca Cola are drunk each year
- There are some 450,000 trees, shrubs and plants
- 5,000,000 flowers are planted every year

Production in action

Background image © Disney

© Disney

Walt Disney

Norman Blood?
By a happy and much-publicised coincidence, Walt Disney's ancestry was French. The name 'Disney' is alleged to come from the Normandy coastal village of Isigny-sur-Mer. After the Norman Conquest of England in 1066, Hughes d'Isigny and his son Robert settled there. Gradually the name became abbreviated and Anglicised. One branch of the family is still in Lincolnshire, having kept the more Gallic spelling D'Isney. But Walt's forebears emigrated to Ireland in the 17th century, and from there Arundel Elias Disney and his brother Robert set sail for North America in 1834. Walt's father was actually born in Canada; his mother came from Ohio. It is a tenuous link, but there is at least some justification for the company's claim that France is the natural home of any European version of a Disneyland® Park.

Walt's name lives on at Walt Disney Studios®

Walter Elias Disney was born in Chicago, Illinois, in 1901, the fourth of five children in a family of slender means. His father was a struggling building contractor whose varied enterprises consistently failed. When they did, the family doggedly moved on, first to Marceline, then to Kansas City, Missouri. Walt's unsettled upbringing gave him only a rudimentary education, and he spent his spare time living on his wits, delivering newspapers door-to-door and hawking sodas on trains. During a brief stint of ambulance-driving in France at the end of World War I (he was too young to join up), he first exercised his artistic talents commercially, painting camouflage helmets and adding fake bullet holes. After the war Walt returned to Kansas City and found a job drawing for an advertising agency. There he met a talented Dutch artist, Ub Iwerks, and together they set up a company, Laugh-o-Gram Films. It soon went to the wall but, like all true romantics of his day, Walt was hopelessly hooked on the glamour of celluloid. With a small fistful of dollars, he set off to try his luck in Hollywood, followed by Ub. From then on Walt had little contact with his parents. But he always kept up with his elder brother Roy, with whom he later set up in business to produce short cartoons. In 1925 Walt married Lillian Bounds, who lived with his erratic genius for over 40 years.

After many false starts and financial failures (one of which involved the loss of his prize cartoon character, Oswald the Lucky Rabbit, to an unprincipled distributor),

Walt's big break came in 1928, using a new character called Mickey Mouse. The film was *Steamboat Willie*, the first animated film to use synchronised sound. Mickey's squeaks and sighs were Walt Disney's own. Roy Disney attempted to temper Walt's wilder impulses with sensible financial caution, but Walt, always cavalier about the money side, was an incorrigible enthusiast, an ideas man, a risk-taker. And his instincts were sound. He could spot a good story at a thousand paces (and shamelessly borrow it, if necessary) and then would edit it brilliantly for his own medium. Above all else, he was a maniacal perfectionist. Every last detail had to be right. All his life he worked obsessively hard, even coming dangerously close to a nervous breakdown in 1931.

Slowly the Disney studios began to prosper with full-length animations like *Snow White and the Seven Dwarfs*, *Pinocchio* and *Fantasia*. After World War II the Disney brothers seized the opportunities offered by the new era of television. Their Disneyland® programme (set up, in part, to fund the first Disney Park) was a great success. From animated films, Disney moved on to using live actors in comedies, wildlife pictures and adventure stories like *Treasure Island*. The core of the business was always safe, clean, family entertainment for the post-war era. The films sold like hot cakes.

Walt first dreamt of theme parks in the 1930s, and the Magic Kingdom in California finally opened in 1953. In 1966 his permanent smoker's cough developed a more sinister note, and by December, just a week after his 65th birthday, he was dead – before he could witness the opening of his Florida park.

Few film producers have captured the imagination, influenced so many people, and aroused such loyalty, loathing and passionate interest as Walt Disney. More than 30 years after his death, debate still rages over the influence of his work – even more over the colossal empire he created to perpetuate it. Through this he has achieved a strangely alarming immortality. So, too, has his single most memorable creation: Mickey Mouse, now over 70 years old.

© Disney

War Effort

In 1918, Walt tried to enlist for military service but was rejected because he was under age (16 years old). Instead he joined the Red Cross and was posted to France. There he spent a year driving a Red Cross ambulance, which was painted, not with camouflage, but with Disney cartoons.

Mickey Mouse

Mickey Mouse made his screen debut in 1928, in the first sound cartoon *Steamboat Willie*. Created by Walt Disney and originally called Mortimer, it was Disney's wife Lillian who suggested the name Mickey as less pretentious. *Steamboat Willie* was a blockbusting success and Mickey Mouse was soon a household name. He was to become a symbol of American optimism, resourcefulness and energy.

The popularity of Mickey Mouse grew and the 1930s saw his 'golden age'. No less that 87 cartoons were made by Disney during that time and new characters emerged who would also become world famous, such as Minnie Mouse, Pluto, Goofy and Donald Duck. In 1940 came the feature film *Fantasia* starring Mickey, with animation techniques way ahead of their time. The stereophonic sound too, was revolutionary.

The world's most famous mouse played his part in the war effort, even to the extent that the password of the Allied forces on D-Day 1944 was 'Mickey Mouse'. During the 1940s and 50s there were fewer Mickey Mouse films with other characters coming to the fore. However Mickey hit the small screen and the Mickey Mouse Club became the most successful children's TV show ever. In subsequent years more children have enjoyed the New Mickey Mouse Club and a third generation of 'Mouseketeers' were seen on the new Disney channel launched in 1989.

Mickey Mouse has played a very important part in the development of the Disney Parks, his first outing was in 1955. He is now seen in both of the US Theme Parks, in Tokyo Disneyland and Disneyland® Resort Paris, where he donned a beret for the opening ceremony.

Mickey Mouse abounds

Mickey Mouse appears on much Disney merchandise

14

Background

In the 1930s Walt began imagining how he could improve on the dreary theme parks he took his daughters to see, but it was only after the war that his obsession developed to fever pitch. At that time amusement parks were bracketed with funfairs and circuses as tawdry and disreputable places. Walt found it very difficult to convey his vision of a place of fun and fantasy in an orderly, civilised setting. He wanted to create a place where both adults and children could enjoy themselves together and come away feeling better. He wanted themes that reflected his Utopian faith in technological progress and the future, a haven in which the archetypal American virtues of pluck and innocence could flourish.

In 1955 Disneyland® Park (also known as 'the Magic Kingdom'), the world's first Theme Park, opened at Anaheim, in Orange County, California. Roy refused to let Walt have the money to build it; he had to cash in his life insurance. But the enterprise succeeded, and the world flocked to see it. Walt began to dream of other Theme Parks, his ambitions growing like beanstalks for a brave new world – a model of planning and innovative lifestyles.

A second site was chosen: the ill-drained acres of central Florida, another 'Orange County'. Quietly the land was purchased on Disney's behalf at knock-down prices through various agencies. Sadly, Walt Disney never lived to see his Floridian dream realised. It was left to his heirs to construct Walt Disney World Resort from the blueprint. This second Disney Park complex opened in Orlando in 1971, much larger and more ambitious than anything in California. Twelve years later, in 1983, another Disneyland® Park appeared in Tokyo. Soon afterwards, a talented new chief executive Michael Eisner, recruited from Paramount, was setting a firm course for the floundering Disney empire, which for several years after its founder's death had seemed to lose its way. Throughout the 1980s the Theme Parks boomed, and revenues from television and merchandising soared. By the middle of the decade plans for a European park were firmly on the drawing board.

Intellectuals have levelled criticism at the anodyne, sanitised qualities of the Disney message, typically declaring it a 'sickening blend of cheap formulas packaged to sell', and a symptom of a kind of infantilism at the heart of the American psyche. In Michael Eisner, Disney's current chieftain, the company seems to have found Walt's true successor, someone with the same unerring instinct for mass-market taste.

The Disney Ethos
Disney values are decent and clean-living. In his many films, and in the Theme Parks, Walt Disney's touching optimism and trust in the goodness of humanity reign supreme (odd in a man who, by all accounts, trusted no one in business). Disney Theme Parks are worlds of happy endings and moral certainties. They are simplistic stuff by the cynical standards of the early 21st century – but they are still popular and, on the surface, seem harmless enough, even charmingly naïve.

© Disney

Character Tips

The Disney characters want you to have the best possible experience with them. Don't force children up to a character that they feel uncomfortable with; the characters are happy to spend some time making a child feel more at ease.

Most characters can sign autograph books, although if a character signals with its hands or paws when handing them a book, they are probably asking for something to be done (open the book, give the pen first). Make sure you have a 'clean' page opened ready to sign; test the pen works, is turned on and the cap is removed. Characters can hear and see, and most enjoy communicating with guests. They love it if you are wearing a piece of clothing with them on it or are holding a stuffed animal.

Imagineers

Any operation on the scale of a Disney Park requires colossal planning and co-operative effort, but just how much goes on behind the scenes may surprise you. A whole workforce of Disney employees called 'Imagineers' devotes its time and energy to inventing and realising the attractions. These artists and technicians are the ones who make illusion reality, working with models and micro-cameras, experimenting with innumerable materials, designs and ideas, studying every last detail for authen-ticity. It is a serious business: careers have been made and broken over the height of some of the buildings. The complexity of all this is fascinating, though most of the illusions are hidden or barely perceived by the vast majority of visitors. When you enter Disneyland® Park, notice how far away the castle seems as you look down Main Street, U.S.A. Why do some of the other buildings seem so accessible? It is all done with clever angles and techniques called 'forced perspective'. Upper storeys are often rather smaller than their proper size, with every architectural detail carefully scaled down. These illusions are just 3-D versions of the kinds of things Disney constantly practised in his films. What the eye sees is not necessarily what is really there, as any animation specialist knows.

Audio–Animatronics®

This Disney-patented system of animating figures (animals, plants, birds and robots as well as humans) has now reached levels of great technical sophistication, and some amazingly lifelike effects can be created. Among striking examples of this new technology are the rowdy pirates in the Pirates of the Caribbeam attraction in Adventureland, and the robots in Visionarium of Discoveryland. Best of all, without a doubt, is the wonderful dragon that lurks beneath the Sleeping Beauty Castle.

Cast Members

Anywhere else, these people would be called Theme Park staff. But here they are the cast – everyone from that fellow sweeping up spilt popcorn to Sleeping Beauty herself. The whole park is a theatrical performance. How do they rehearse for that relentless PR exercise, constantly smiling and helpful? They go to university! The Disney University, where appropriate cheerful responses are drilled into prospective members, and deviant tendencies like tattoos, red nail polish and facial hair are rigorously drilled out. However, some concessions have been made to French fashion: red lipstick may be worn, tastefully. And who are you? You are the guests at this show.

Strict Dress Code

Before 2000 male Cast Members at Disneyland and Walt Disney World were not allowed to have beards, moustaches or long hair. Today they can sport neatly trimmed moustaches but they must be grown during the holidays. From July 2003 the restrictions on male hairstyles were relaxed but must still meet strict specifications. Female Cast Members were forbidden to wear eyeshadow and eyeliner prior to 1994. Up until the late 60s, all men with long hair (including visitors) were refused entry to the parks.

Say hello to Snow White and the Seven Dwarfs

Features of
Disneyland® Resort Paris

Media – Radio, TV, Newpapers

All bedrooms in the Disney hotels at Disneyland® Resort Paris are equipped with cable television, currently receiving five French channels as well as international channels, including BBC World, CNBC and Eurosport, plus three Disney channels, which relay closed-circuit information and Disney films. There are several radio stations, mostly featuring music. A wide variety of foreign newspapers and magazines are available in hotel shops and at the RER station.

It is well worth spending some time familiarising yourself with the layout of Disneyland® Resort Paris and the Parks, particularly if you only have one or two days to see everything. Those hours spent in the Disney Parks will be expensive if you waste time, but if you use them well you will not be disappointed. Study the maps of the Parks, which although not to scale, both show Disney® Village, the parking area and hotels in relation to the Parks.

Disneyland® Resort Paris

Disneyland® Resort Paris covers a total land area of about 1,500 acres (600ha). When you hear that there is still room for development, you realise the gigantic proportions of the whole project! At present the resort includes seven themed Disney hotels, three new Selected hotels, a 27-hole golf course, the Disney® Village entertainment centre, the Disneyland® Park, which alone represents 140 acres (57ha), and the Walt Disney Studios® Park, 62 acres (25ha) at opening stage.

Exit roads from surrounding routes lead smoothly along newly constructed dual carriageways to all parts of the Resort, with all hotels and the main car park clearly signposted from exit 14 of the A4 motorway. For Disney's Davy Crockett Ranch® take exit 13. If you need petrol, you will find it by Disney's Hotel Santa Fe®. From the large visitor's car park (remember in which section you leave your vehicle), covered moving walkways lead to a wide avenue that heads straight for the parks' entrance and

Swimming at Davy Crockett Ranch®

© Disney

ticket offices past the film-set decor of Disney® Village on the left. The entrance gates of the Walt Disney Studios® Park are opposite the glass dome of the RER station. Farther on, beside the unmissable Disneyland® Hotel is the entrance to the Disneyland® Park. If you have a pet, you must leave it at the Animal Care Center next to the parking area, where a service charge applies (▶ Charges). At the end of the moving walkways there is a picnic area. There is a car park for disabled visitors nearer the entrance.

If you arrive by commuter train you will emerge at the Marne-la-Vallée–Chessy RER station, very close to the entrance to both Disney Parks. There is a post office inside the station. Next to it is the TGV-Eurostar station, terminal point of the express link joining all European rail networks.

Several expanses of artificially created water form scenic vistas within the resort area. Lake Disney® is surrounded by three hotels, each representing a typical aspect of the American scene: Disney's Hotel New York®, Disney's Sequoia Lodge® and Disney's Newport Bay Club®. Two more hotels, Disney's Hotel Santa Fe® and Disney's Hotel Cheyenne®, straddle the Rio Grande, a canal northeast of Lake Disney®. There are traffic-free promenades on either side of the water, making the route between the Disney Parks and the Resort Hotels a pleasant walk, but a free shuttle bus is available. Disney's Davy Crockett Ranch®, situated at the heart of a forested area and symbolising the American pioneer spirit, is a 15-minute drive to the Disney Parks (no shuttle bus runs).

Disney® Village

Opposite the RER station is an eye-catching complex that looks like a film set, or rather several contrasting film sets, re-creating the atmosphere of typical American towns: angular metallic structures linked by a cat's cradle of wires tower above ochre-coloured saloons and bars along a wide avenue extending to the edge of Lake Disney®, beyond the huge globe of the deliberately flashy Planet Hollywood restaurant.

During the day the sun glitters on the shiny aluminium and mosaic panels; at night the area is a maze of starry lights rocking to the sound of live concerts all year round. This bold modern structure was designed by Californian architect Frank Gehry and is Disneyland® Resort Paris's principal entertainment centre apart from the Disney Parks. It aims to offer alternative entertainment, eating and shopping facilities to the Parks' visitors during the day and keep them happy after the Parks' gates have closed. It consists of shops, restaurants, bars and various night

Multilingual Staff
Though France is the host country of Disneyland® Resort Paris, both staff and visitors are a great mix of nationalities. French and English are the official languages, and you will find notices, show scripts and so on in both. Many of the staff speak one or more other language, particularly German, Dutch, Spanish or Italian. You will obviously find many French staff. Their communication skills are impressive, but not always completely fluent. It is always appreciated if you are prepared to use a little French and meet your hosts halfway. Apart from language, the mood is American, and the rigorous Disney discipline is imposed. Everyone is neat and tidy, everyone smiles a lot, and everyone wishes you a nice day.

Fastpass®

This free time-saving service is designed to cut waiting times at the following popular attractions.

In Disneyland® Park: Indiana Jones™ and the Temple of Peril: Backwards!, Space Mountain – from the Earth to the Moon, Big Thunder Mountain, Peter Pan's Flight, Star Tours.

In Walt Disney Studios® Park: Rock'n' Roller Coaster starring Aerosmith and Flying Carpets Over Agrabah.

By inserting your Park Ticket into the distributor machine at the entrance of the attraction of your choice, you will receive a ticket for a one hour time slot. If you return to the attraction during this time, you will be able to enter within a short time, thus avoiding the traditional waiting time. You cannot use more than one Fastpass® at one time, Note that this service is subject to availability and it is advisable to visit popular attractions as early as possible.

Planet Hollywood in Disney Village

spots, including a nightclub and the popular Buffalo Bill's Wild West Dinner Show, as well as a Gaumont Cinema that has 15 screens (with a total seating capacity of 3,658; English films are also shown on selected dates). Practical facilities include the tourist information bureau for the Île de France region, an American Express office and a parking area. The Disney® Village complex is open every day and there is no entrance charge except on 31 December.

Disney Parks

A practical approach is necessary if you wish to make the most of a day of non-stop entertainment in the magical world of Disney. Both Parks provide useful services to make sure that you enjoy yourself to the full. Bulky articles you will not need during your visit can be handed in at Guest storage (service charge), situated outside the Disneyland® Park entrance, close to the Guest Relations office, and just inside Walt Disney Studios® Park, next to Studios Services.

Once through the gates, you are ready to begin your journey and will want to get your bearings as quickly as possible; look at the map given to you on arrival: Walt Disney Studios® Park is divided into four distinct production areas starting with the Front Lot, overlooked by the tall water tower. Disneyland® Park is also divided, rather like a pie chart, into five separate thematic areas or lands: beyond Main Street, U.S.A. stretching ahead of you, lies the park's central landmark, Sleeping Beauty Castle, its spindly turrets thrusting into the Île-de-France sky. But once inside the Parks, do not be dazzled by the lure of the 108-ft (33-m)-high Studios Water Tower, or the enchanting Sleeping Beauty Castle. Instead take time to look around Walt Disney Studios® Park's Mediterranean courtyard or Disneyland® Park's turn-of-the-century main square, because here is where you will find some extremely useful facilities and services.

Studio Services (Walt Disney Studios® Park) and City Hall (Disneyland® Park), both situated just inside the gates, are the parks' main information centres and are well worth a visit: they are a convenient meeting place for families and friends, and messages can also be left for them. Guide maps in several languages, Park information, Entertainment programmes, Disabled Guest Guides and information in Braille are available at the desks, where you can also book a room, a restaurant, a dinner-show or a

Do's & Don'ts

Some Do's

- Remember to bring a sweater, light rainwear and to wear comfortable shoes.
- Shoes and shirts must be worn at all times.
- Reduce waiting time by making use of the Fastpass® service (▶ panel 20)
- Children under seven must be accompanied by an adult.
- Get a hand-stamp if you leave either Disney Park so that you can get back in again later, and make sure you have your Park Ticket(s) with you.
- Check on closing times.
- Pick up an Entertainment Program from City Hall in Disneyland® Park or from Studio Services in Walt Disney Studios® Park.
- Life is easier if you use a credit card. Visa, Mastercard or American Express are widely accepted. Guests staying at a Disneyland® Resort Paris hotel will be given a chargecard that can be used within the Resort.
- Visit the tourist office next to the RER station if you are thinking about touring outside the Resort (tel: 01 60 43 33 33, daily 9AM–10PM).

© Disney

Make the most of the FASTPASS®

© Disney

& Some Don'ts

- Smoking, eating and drinking are not allowed inside attractions and in queuing areas. Restaurants are divided into smoking and non-smoking sections. A picnic area located between Guest Parking and the Disney Parks Entrance is intended for guests bringing their own food.
- No pets, except guide dogs, are allowed to enter the Parks. They may be left at the Animal Care Center near the car park on production of a certificate of health, or verification of vaccination. A service charge applies (▶ Charges).
- Do not leave personal belongings unattended.
- No flash photography or video taping are allowed inside the attractions.

Background image © Disney

Tight Budget

Taking a family to Disneyland® Resort Paris is by no means a budget holiday option but there are ways to cut the costs.

Extras can mount up – all the ice creams and soft drinks, the T-shirts and mouse ears – you may have to restrain from impulse buys. Families and friends can save money by staying in just one room – most Disneyland® Resort Paris hotel bedrooms can accommodate parties of four. It is cheaper to stay in a local motel or small hotel nearby, but not actually in, the resort. Choose counter-service cafés for snacks, rather than more expensive table-service restaurants, or you can bring your own and eat it in the picnic area outside the Theme Parks. Consider buying a three-day passport Disney Park Entrance Ticket, which reduces the adult daily entrance charge by about 25 per cent. Take some light raingear with you to avoid having to spend money on a Mickey Mouse poncho, if it rains. Above all, keep your children away from video games arcades. All the machines eat up euros at a fearsome rate.

Character Tea; check the times of the shows and parades on offer in the Parks; change your money at the American Express Foreign Currency Exchange; or make reservations for a guided walking tour of either or both parks (one-hour tours of Walt Disney Studios® Park, two-hour tours of Disneyland® Park).

If it's a pushchair or wheelchair you need, then you can hire one by the day near Studio Services in Walt Disney Studios® Park or across Town Square from City Hall in Disneyland® Park; a padlock is useful to keep your pushchair safe while you take young children on rides. Note that Cast Members are not available to accompany guests in wheelchairs or to look after children while their parents enjoy attractions that are unsuitable for young children. However, Disneyland® Resort Paris has found a way to alleviate adult frustration in this case: it's called 'baby switch' and it allows parents to do the attraction without having to stand in the queue twice (information from the Cast Members at the entrance to the attraction).

The Lost and Found office is next to Studio Services at the entrance to Walt Disney Studios® Park and at City Hall in Disneyland® Park.

Before you leave the Town Square to explore the rest of Disneyland® Park, bear in mind that it is a good place to watch the Parade and take pictures from different angles as the floats slowly make their way round the square; a spot is reserved for people in wheelchairs in front of Ribbons & Bows Hat Shop.

Now that you have everything you need and are in the right mood to make the most of your visit, you can uncover the magic of cinema at Walt Disney Studios® Park. Or at Disneyland® Park, you can walk down Main Street, U.S.A., hop on one of the nostalgic vehicles bound for Central Plaza or embark on a journey round Disneyland® Park aboard one of the steam trains of the Disneyland® Railroad. When you get to Central Plaza, you will see the Plaza Gardens Restaurant on your right; next to it are three more services that might prove useful at some time during your visit: the First Aid Center, the Baby Care Center and the Lost Children Office. All three are also located behind Studio Services in Walt Disney Studios® Park.

Should you need to withdraw cash while you are inside one of the Disney Parks, you will find automatic cash dispensers next to Studio Services and at Backlot Express Restaurant in Walt Disney Studios® Park, as well as in the arcades parallel to Main Street, U.S.A., in Adventureland and in Discoveryland inside Disneyland® Park.

Opening times, operating procedures and so on are subject to change without notice, and it is always advisable to check with Guest Relations for up-to-date information. Occasionally attractions may be closed for technical reasons (such as safety checks).

Make the Most of Your Visit

Your action plan depends very much on what sort of ticket you have (there are 1–5 day tickets available). The chances are that if you have booked through a tour operator you will have unlimited entrance to both Disney Parks included for the duration of your stay.

If you have bought just a one-day entrance ticket, you will first have to decide which Disney Park you want to visit. If you choose Walt Disney Studios® Park, your ticket also entitles you to enter Disneyland® Park after 5PM. If you prefer to spend the day in Disneyland® Park, you will have to tackle the Park like a military exercise if you want to see it all. Get there early and head for the popular rides first (Big Thunder Mountain or Space Mountain), making the most of slack periods (for example, during mealtimes, the parades or in the evening). You will obviously get more value out of your ticket if you choose a time when Disneyland® Park stays open late (in summer, or at peak holiday times). A useful time-saver is the free FASTPASS® available at five attractions in Disneyland® Park and at two attractions in Walt Disney Studios® Park (► panel 20).

With a three day entrance ticket, you have more time to experience the two Parks. In addition, you can take a rest whenever you like, and do the things you like best more than once. If you are staying at Disneyland® Resort Paris for several days, it is a good idea to have a break from the Parks at some point to get in touch with reality again – tour an area of France, or go to Paris. Then come back and have another day. Most people can have a good two days' fun out of Disneyland® Park; keen theme-parkers like to stay even longer. What if you hate it once you get inside? Well, it is true that not everyone likes Theme Parks. The chances are, though, that you will want more time than you actually have available.

If you do buy a three-day ticket, do not try to see the

Seasonal Events
Each season throughout the year brings a different theme to Disneyland® Resort Paris. Mist-filled mornings and rich autumn skies produce Disney's Halloween Festival, while Christmas traditions such as falling snowflakes and Father Christmas inspire the winter season. Come the spring it is carnival time and summer always has a surprise or two waiting.

Buffalo Bill's Wild West Show, Disney Village

Child Facilities

Child facilities are well publicised throughout the Parks. There is a Baby Care Center in Main Street U.S.A. (Disneyland® Park) or behind Studio Services (Walt Disney Studios® Park) where nappies can be changed, bottles warmed and basic necessities purchased. Pushchairs (strollers) can be rented for use within the Parks in Town Square (Disneyland® Park) or near Studio Services (Walt Disney Studios® Park). There are no restrictions on pushchairs being brought into the Parks. Lost children will be taken to the Lost Children Office and looked after until you find them. And if after enjoying a day with the family in the Parks, parents want to have a night out on their own, Disneyland® Resort Paris is certainly the place to stay since all of the Disneyland® Resort Paris hotels provide baby-sitting services.

whole of either Park on day one. Save some of the excitement for your next visit. In Disneyland® Park visit Main Street, U.S.A., the Sleeping Beauty Castle, Fantasyland and Discoveryland on day one, and then go to Frontierland and Adventureland on day two. You can try out your favourite rides again, have a relaxing lunch, look round all the shops, or even leave the Disney Park for a nap or a swim at your hotel on day three. It is particulary important to prevent children from becoming overtired. And if the weather is hot, make sure they get enough to drink and are protected from the sun. No two children react in quite the same way to Disneyland® Resort Paris Park's attractions. Most take them in a matter-of-fact way, and some are completely blasé. Others get wildly excited, a few frightened or sick. It is quite difficult to assess what may alarm a child. Very young ones may find the spooks in Phantom Manor, the eerier sections of Pirates of the Caribbean, or the Wicked Queen Snow White and the Seven Dwarfs quite perturbing.

Here is a brief run-down of attractions, showing which ones are best for which people

Young Children

Very young children will best enjoy the rides on Main Street, U.S.A, the Sleeping Beauty Castle and Fantasyland with its fairytale theme rides: Peter Pan's Flight, Pinocchio's Fantastic Journey, Snow White and the Seven Dwarfs, Casey Jr – le Petit Train du Cirque or Storybook Land; you could also try your luck with Alice's Curious Labyrinth and 'it's a small world'. Take them for a gentle boat ride round the Rivers of the Far West, and visit Critter Corral to see some real live animals. Make sure they get a chance to meet Mickey Mouse at some point, too. They will probably enjoy the Swiss Family Robinson Treehouse and a ride on one of the steam trains. See the shows at Fantasy Festival Stage, Chaparral Theatre or the Royal Castle Stage. Also, catch the daytime parade, even if you do not want to keep the children up late enough to see the Fantillusion Parade (on certain dates through the year).

Older Children

Boys usually prefer Frontierland, Adventureland, and Discoveryland, so go to them when you have seen the Sleeping Beauty Castle. After a few rides they may want to try absolutely everything, even 'baby rides' like Dumbo the Flying Elephant and Lancelot's Carousel, but they may scorn Fantasyland's younger appeal at first.

A Spot of Adrenalin

Frontierland attractions include a runaway mine train at Big Thunder Mountain and a visit to Phantom Manor. Have a go at shooting bank robbers at the Rustler Roundup Shootin' Gallery (you will need extra euros for this). In Adventureland try the rope and plank bridges, and Indiana Jones™ and the Temple of Peril: Backwards. In Discoveryland go for maximum throttle in a 'car of the future' on Autopia (the race-track), pilot a spaceship in Orbitron, or take a ride through outer space in Star Tours and Space Mountain. Volunteer for Honey, I Shrunk the Audience, an amazing shrinking experience with spine-chilling visual and tactile effects. In the evening, be sure to catch the fireworks (seasonal only). The last few seconds are extremely exciting.

Restrictions

No children under three are allowed to ride on Star Tours; none under one on Dumbo the Flying Elephant, Orbitron, Peter Pan's Flight and Casey Jr – le Petit Train du Cirque. There are height restrictions on Big Thunder Mountain, Indiana Jones™ and the Temple of Peril: Backwards, Space Mountain and Autopia in Disneyland® Park and on Rock'n' Roller Coaster starring Aerosmith in Walt Disney Studios® Park. If you suffer from motion sickness you may be wise to avoid off avoiding Big Thunder Mountain, Space Mountain, Orbitron and the Mad Hatter's Tea Cups, (and Rock'n'Roller Coaster in Walt Disney Studios® Park) though an excess of ice-cream is usually more to blame for the queasiness. The Visionarium can also be mildly disturbing, as the pictures on the screen give a convincing illusion of motion. Honey, I Shrunk the Audience is fairly loud and intense. If you are pregnant, or have a weak back, heart or neck, avoid jolting rides.

© Disney

Indulge in time travel and space travel at Discoveryland

THE 10 ESSENTIALS

If you only have a short time to visit Disneyland® Resort Paris and would like to take home unforgettable memories, here are the essentials:

- **Watch the Disney night-time parade** with its twinkling lights and favourite Disney characters.

- **Ride Space Mountain** in Discoveryland for the ultimate in galactic travel. Blast off from the rocket ship for a trip into space.

- **Big Thunder Mountain** in Frontierland is a must for thrill seekers as you hurtle through the rocky landscape and deep into a mine.

- **Experience a high speed thrill** on Indiana Jones™ and the Temple of Peril: Backwards, a roller coaster to get the adrenalin going. The ride, in Adventureland, finishes with a dramatic loop-the-loop.

- **Pirates of the Caribbean,** located in Adventureland, is one of the most realistic attractions in the Park. It has great special effects, full of swashbuckling adventure.

- **Sleeping Beauty Castle** in Fantasyland is every child's interpretation of fairyland and a main landmark of the Park.

- **Undergo a 3-D 'shrinking' experience** by watching Honey I Shrunk the Audience in Discoveryland. A host of special effects are employed for a really original sensation.

Disaster strikes in Catastrophe Canyon, Walt Disney Studios® Park

- **Take in a show** from the schedule of spectacular performances that include The Legend of the Lion King and the Tarzan™ Encounter.

- **Studio Tram Tour: Behind the Magic** featuring Catastrophe Canyon at the Walt Disney Studios® Park is not just a tour round the studio; stand by for an exciting trip.

- **Check out Moteurs Action Stunt Show Spectacular** in Back Lot at Walt Disney Studios® Park for the best in cinema stunts with cars, motorbikes, jet skis and more all in action.

© Disney

Background image © Disney

© Disney

What to See

Above: *a rope and plank bridge leads to Adventure Isle, Disneyland® Park*

Disneyland® Park

Disneyland® Park oozes on a grand scale the Disney magic that has enchanted several generations of children and the young at heart. Here mesmerising characters welcome visitors to a land where dreams come true, where make-believe is real, where imagination becomes reality. Feel the excitement and laughter as you stroll down Main Street, U.S.A., gateway to Disneyland® Park's four other themed lands, Frontierland, Adventureland, Fantasyland and Discoverland. Through shows, parades and thrilling rides for all ages relive the legendary era of the Wild West, encompass an adventure through the Middle East, African jungles and tropical islands, see your favourite fairy tales come to life and discover the futuristic sensation waiting at every turn.

Take a spin on the Mad Hatter's Teacups, Fantasyland

Main Street, U.S.A.

The scene is set by the flamboyant Victorian splendour of the Disneyland® Hotel straddling the entrance gates, even before you pass through the turnstiles into Station Plaza. Once visitors emerge into Town Square from Main Street Station, they are in small-town America at about the turn of the 20th century (as those of us who never saw it like to imagine it might have been). It is a world of gas-lamps and horse-drawn streetcars, decorative lettering and absurdly pretty architecture, all in the colours of Italian ice cream. Each minutely detailed façade in Town Square and Main Street, U.S.A. is different, but the ornate balustrades and barge-boards, pediments and parapets seem to be in perfect scale and harmony. This is a magnificent piece of deception by the Disney Imagineers – the top storeys are subtly graduated in size, so that the Sleeping Beauty Castle appears much farther away than it really is. All the street furniture – lamp-posts, letter-boxes, litter-bins, fire hydrants – have been carefully designed to suit the period.

© Disney

©DISNEY

Main Street, U.S.A. is the orientation centre of the Park, where you can ask for information, store belongings, hire wheelchairs or pushchairs, book guided tours, find out about lost property (or lost people), and generally warm to the Disneyland® Park mood as marching bands keep up a brisk tempo. The rest of Main Street, U.S.A. is mostly devoted to shops and eating places. In Town Square there are neat municipal gardens, park benches and a gazebo, where you can board one of the trundling period vehicles to transport you down Main Street, U.S.A, which links Town Square with the hub of the Park, Central Plaza, beside which the Sleeping Beauty Castle stands. From here you can choose which of the lands to see next. If you prefer, you can take a train from Main Street Station, located up steps just inside Town Square, and either go on a complete circuit of the Park to get your bearings, or get off at Frontierland, Fantasyland or Discoveryland.

TIP

If it is raining, head for the arcades at either side of Main Street, U.S.A.

A horse-drawn streetcar on Main Street, U.S.A.

ONE WAY TRANSPORTATION

First port of call – the information centre

TIP

Do not become mesmerised by all the shops and balloon-sellers unless you have plenty of time. If you spend too long on them, you will not have time to see the rest of the Park.

Discovery Arcade – an entertaining place to shelter from the the rain

What to See on Main Street, U.S.A.

ARCADES ⭐

There are two covered passageways on either side of Main Street, U.S.A. with rear access to the shops and restaurants. Inside they are beautifully decorated in fin-de-siècle style, with wrought-iron work and pretty gas lamps. Liberty Arcade, on the left side of Main Street, U.S.A. as you face the castle, contains an exhibition about the Statue of Liberty, with plans, drawings, photographs and the Statue of Liberty Tableau. This is a diorama about the unveiling of the monument – a diplomatic touch by Disney, emphasising Franco-American friendship and collaboration. The inaugural ceremony took place in New York harbour in 1886. The 108ft- (33m) high statue by the French sculptor Frédéric-Auguste Bartholdi is made up of bronze strips fixed to a steel frame designed by Gustave Eiffel, who made the headlines barely three years later when his famous tower was inaugurated for the 1889 World Exhibition. 'Liberty enlightening the World' was a gift from the French people to the American people to celebrate the centenary of the American War of Independence and French involvement in it. Discovery Arcade, on the right side of Main Street, U.S.A. features cabinets displaying various inventions from the early 20th-century flying machines to strange sporting equipment. Fun to look at if you have lots of spare time.

© Disney

DISNEYLAND RAILROAD

These charming steam engines chug around the perimeter of the Disney Park, stopping at Main Street, U.S.A., Frontierland Depot, and Fantasyland and Discoveryland stations. Disneyland® Park would not be complete without an old train or two, for nostalgic railways were one of Walt's abiding passions. He even had a complete track with scaled-down steam engine and carriages built in his garden! At Disneyland® Park there are four individual, authentically styled locomotives, all beautifully painted and fitted and evoking the great railroad days of late-19th-century America. One is a Presidential Train of the type used by government officials, another a pioneering Wild West Train, the third an East Coast Excursion Train. The fourth is called *Eureka* as a reminder of the famous cry which echoed throughout America in 1849 and started the Gold Rush. The engines were manufactured by Welsh boilermakers with every detail carefully in place: whistles, smoke-stacks, cowcatchers and shiny brass fittings. These engines genuinely run on steam produced by water going through a diesel boiler, a departure from authenticity deliberately made by the pollution-conscious Disney team. Each engine fills up with water from the Frontierland tank every hour or so. The carriages are open on one side, giving good views of the Park. Each train can take about 270 passengers, and one arrives about every 10 minutes; it takes 20 minutes to go right round the Disney Park.

On the journey between Main Street Station and Frontierland Depot the train passes through Grand Canyon Diorama (► 38).

DISNEY'S PARADES

The Disney parades are a major attraction and a real focal point of Main Street, U.S.A. They are elaborate, colourful spectacles like carnival processions, with lots of floats. They start near Fantasyland and proceed down Main Street, U.S.A.

You will find the area very crowded. Stake out a good vantage point in advance. If you time a visit to Walt's – an American Restaurant very carefully and are lucky enough to get a window table (very expensive, though) you should get a good view of the parades from the upper floor. Views from the other Main Street, U.S.A. restaurants are distant, or will probably be blocked by kerb-side spectators, but you may be lucky in Plaza Gardens. Disney Theme Parks are famous for their parades, and Disneyland® Park's change regularly. The ImagiNations Parade, running through 2000, was the biggest, most imaginative parade

> **TIP**
>
> If you are particularly keen to see any attraction, restaurant or show, check at City Hall what is available.

> **TIP**
>
> Main Street Station is generally very busy, so join the Disneyland® Railroad at one of the other stations instead (in Frontierland, Fantasyland or Discoveryland).

*Hop aboard the
Disneyland Railroad*

© Disney

yet, featuring huge floats four storeys high. The Princess Parade takes place daily at 3PM, on a more or less regular basis – except when the Christmas Parade takes over with a special guest from Lapland! It is a classic Disney Parade bringing to life scenes from everyone's favourite animated films. Clowns, jugglers, costumed dancers and Disney Characters liven up the procession by fooling around among the crowd and enticing young children to join them.

By night the spectacle is even more remarkable. The Disney Fantillusion Parade is definitely worth catching, as it includes some wonderful creations. As if all this is not enough, the evening's entertainment sometimes ends with a remarkable fireworks display. Guests should note that Disney's Fantillusional Parade and fireworks are seasonal only.

VEHICLES ★

Other modes of transportation available in Main Street, U.S.A. date from the same era as the trains. These vehicles are not genuine antiques, but they are authentically re-created by master craftsmen. Among them are horse-drawn streetcars pulled by patient Shires and Percherons, an early double-decker Omnibus, a chauffeured limousine, a fire truck and a police wagon. Guests can queue up in Town Square for a brief ride to Central Plaza in whichever vehicle is running. But don't be deceived by Main Street Motors that, in spite of its name and the reconditioned genuine vintage car on display inside, sells souvenirs based on Disney and animated films.

TIP

Riding a streetcar is a good way of avoiding temptation in Boardwalk Candy Palace.

Frontierland

This is the largest of the five lands, distinguished from the others by a Wild West theme, large expanses of water, and a spectacular Arizona-style landscape. Here there is one of the Park's most exciting attractions, Big Thunder Mountain, and two different kinds of boat trip are offered. Like Main Street, U.S.A., Frontierland has a clear architectural theme, based on an imaginary Wild West town of the late 1800s called Thunder Mesa. If parts of Frontierland look surprisingly authentic, that is because they are. Disney Imagineers collected real antiques from many states in the US, and transported them here for special effect.

©DISNEY

There is something for everyone at Frontierland. Even if you are not a Wild West enthusiast, you will almost certainly be impressed by the drama of this entirely artificial landscape, created from flat, unpromising terrain. The Disney Imagineers excelled themselves here, recreating the vastness of the American West to such an extent that, looking at the wild canyons and ochre-coloured sandstone monoliths, you will imagine yourself travelling through the Rocky Mountains. Pioneer fever will no doubt grip you as you step into the Lucky Nugget Saloon to have a meal and watch a real French cancan show!

> **TIP**
>
> If it is raining you can walk under cover to Frontierland, from Liberty Arcade in Main Street, U.S.A. or from the Adventureland Bazaar.

The Lucky Nugget restaurant

You can approach Frontierland from several directions. The usual way is from Central Plaza, through Fort Comstock, the log stockade. If you are going around the Park anti-clockwise, you can approach Frontierland from Adventureland, and watch how cleverly the pirate scene fades to cowboys and Indians. You can also come by train (they chug clockwise round the Park). On the way between Main Street Station and Frontierland Depot, trains pass through Grand Canyon Diorama (▶ 38).

© Disney

Experience the thrill of Big Thunder Mountain

What to See in Frontierland

BIG THUNDER MOUNTAIN ●●●

The most exciting and conspicuous attraction in Frontierland, and one of the best in Disneyland® Park. It may take a little while to pluck up enough courage to visit this ride, so wild are the screams from those riding it. But do not miss this experience. It is reached by taking a roller-coaster ride aboard a runaway mine train. The track passes through a carefully reconstructed landscape, similar to that found in Arizona or Utah, particularly around Monument Valley. The rocky set rises to 119ft (36m), and immense pains have been taken to achieve an impression of age in the mine buildings by staining, bleaching and rusting.

The ride is certainly wilder than at Orlando. What makes the former so good is its mystery factor. Unlike most roller-coasters, the runaway mine train at Big Thunder Mountain is unpredictable and once the train goes into the mine-workings anything can happen.

Even the queuing is creatively arranged for this attraction – the tightly coiled lines shuffle steadily through the extremely realistic reconstruction of the Big Thunder Mountain Mining Company's headquarters. Tension builds up as the point of no return is reached. The train pulls away, then plunges into a shaft and the caverns of the mine-workings, full of stalactites and glowing bats' eyes. Hurtling through a mining camp and a pine-forest, where possoms swing from the branches, the train then dives into a dynamite explosion. The roof caves in, briefly revealing huge veins of gold. The train plunges on, this time facing a new danger from the flooding river, which is

© Disney

washing away part of the track. Eventually the exhilarated passengers are brought safely back to base, chortling with delight, eager to do it all again.

This popular attraction is certainly one that can stand a repeat performance, as it is difficult to take in all the details in one go. Children under three (or below a certain height) are not allowed to go on the ride; nor should anyone consider going on it if they are pregnant, or have neck or back problems.

CRITTER CORRAL

Enclosure of a typical Western ranch near Frontierland Depot (railway station) where visitors can see and pet some real animals.

FORT COMSTOCK AND LEGENDS OF THE
WILD WEST ✪✪

Guarding the main entrance to Frontierland, Fort Comstock is a replica of the sort of log stockade constructed by early pioneers as a defence against Indian attack. Inside, a series of picturesque scenes depict life in the American West with the help of legendary types of characters immortalised in famous westerns; there is the gold prospector called 'Forty-Niner', because of the 1849 Gold Rush, the outlaw, the lawman, as well as the larger than life characters, Buffalo Bill and Davy Crockett.

The Indian Camp outside gives a vivid account of the Native Americans' traditional way of life and visitors can admire authentic Cheyenne handicraft. The tour also offers a splendid overall view of Frontierland and the opportunity to meet a real Cheyenne Indian chief.

TIP

Big Thunder Mountain and (to a lesser extent) Phantom Manor are major attractions where queues are likely to be long, so try to visit them early, late, or at meal or parade times. Note that Big Thunder Mountain is included on the FASTPASS® (▶ panel 20).

Phantom Manor – not for the faint-hearted

GRAND CANYON DIORAMA

Although this attraction is located within Frontierland, it can only be seen from the Disneyland® Railroad (trains depart regularly from Main Street, U.S.A., Frontierland, Fantasyland and Discoveryland stations).

Trains enter a 262-ft (80m) tunnel, in which the scenery of the Grand Canyon is re-created, subtly lit to give the impression that the journey along the canyon rim takes not just a few minutes, but an entire day from sunrise to sunset. Guests first encounter ancient Indian cliff dwellings hollowed from the canyon walls, and then a forest in which a herd of deer is grazing. Other wildlife can be seen, too: a fox stalking a pack rat; a rattlesnake coiled on a ledge; raccoons and squirrels; and a cougar and her cubs by a cave. A thunderstorm gathers and, as a rainbow forms, antelope descend into the canyon. The diorama consists of a huge mural, with many animals and species of vegetation. Lighting, music and sound effects all play a part. As the train emerges from the tunnel passengers find they have reached the Rivers of the Far West, with Big Thunder Mountain beyond.

PHANTOM MANOR

The eerie, ramshackle mansion of Phantom Manor was built by one of Thunder Mesa's early settlers, who became rich during the Gold Rush. But tragedy struck when his only daughter disappeared on her wedding day. The house was left empty and fell into decay. You can believe this if you like – but isn't that a candle inside?

Guests bound for Phantom Manor are ushered into a strange circular room by sinister hosts. The doors shut and the walls change shape. Those innocent-looking pictures take on horrifying new dimensions as the floor stretches. Guests then descend to board a 'Doom Buggy' for the journey through the house. Mocking laughter, beating door-knockers, creaking hinges, and a clock tolling 13 start the mystery tour. A ghostly bride appears sobbing at intervals, while a medium's head is visible in a crystal ball. One of the best special effects is the holograms, which are used for the wedding feast. Guests dance and fade, and a parade of ghosts, ghouls and skeletons follows before the passengers are released from their ordeal.

Outside in the fresh air, guests emerge near Boot Hill, the cemetery overlooking the Rivers of the Far West, which is full of amusing gravestones. Some are even, by Disney standards, slightly risqué: 'Sacred to the Memory of Rev. Jared Bates, who died Aug 6 1862. Erected by the girls of The Lucky Nugget Saloon'.

RIVER ROGUE KEELBOATS ✪✪

These boats are modelled on the ones used in a Disney television film called *Davy Crockett and the River Pirates*. They are diesel-powered, 40ft (12m) long and hold about 40 passengers each. Unlike the stately paddlewheel river-boats, which follow a fixed course, the keelboats weave in and out, and you may find yourself perilously close to the rocks at some point. The keelboats leave from a dock at Smuggler's Cove (subject to weather conditions).

All sorts of spooks hang out at Phantom Manor

*Play at being a cowboy in
Frontierland*

RUSTLER ROUNDUP SHOOTIN' GALLERY

This is fun. Instead of bullets, the guns fire electronic impulses at a Wild West scene containing 74 animated targets: among them cacti, a windmill and a dynamite shack. (The only human one is a peeping Tom.) If you hit them, all kinds of things happen. There is a charge for this attraction to prevent people from hogging the guns all day.

THUNDER MESA RIVERBOAT LANDING
(PADDLEWHEEL RIVERBOATS)

The careful landscaping and detailing of the various sections of the Rivers of the Far West make the paddle-wheel riverboat trip round Big Thunder Mountain quite an adventure. On the way you will see Smuggler's Cove; Wilderness Island, a green oasis where Joe sleeps in a rocking-chair, his dog barking at passing boats; Settlers' Landing, a dry dock with supplies for pioneering

homesteaders; an abandoned wagon with two skeletal oxen in the sand; and Geyser Plateau, where steaming, bubbling, mineral-rich water jets over the bones of dinosaurs. The scenery evokes the landscape of the Wild West, with its grand geological formations (rock bridges and canyons) and high desert plateaux known as mesas.

From Thunder Mesa Riverboat Landing near the Silver Spur Steakhouse visitors can choose between two riverboats: *Mark Twain* and *Molly Brown*. They are both authentically reconstructed paddlewheel riverboats of the type that plied the Mississippi and Sacramento rivers at the time of the Gold Rush. One is a stern-wheeler, the other a side-wheeler. They were both built specifically for Disneyland® Park. The vessels are ornately fitted with mahogany and brass, with teak decks and comfortable upholstery. Each boat carries about 400 passengers, and their nostalgic voyage lasts around 15 minutes.

© Disney

Stately paddlewheel riverboats ply the Rivers of the Far West

41

Adventureland

This is one of the most attractive parts of Disneyland® Park. In contrast to Frontierland, here there is no geographic unity since the inspiration of the Disney Imagineers was drawn from three continents – the islands of the Caribbean, the African desert and the Asian jungle. Yet Adventureland is pleasantly landscaped in a natural style, with water, islands, rocks and lots of vegetation, including a bamboo grove. In addition, it has two of the most popular rides, a collection of genuinely interesting shops in its North African bazaar, and several of the nicest eating places. In all, it has a lot going for it, and should appeal to any age group.

©DISNEY

One of the two main attractions, Pirates of the Caribbean, is complex and technically sophisticated – yet Adventureland as a whole has an air of innocence about it in keeping with the original spirit of Disney. Its pleasures are simpler than much of the Disney Park – climbing treehouses, walking wobbly bridges, exploring caves. The central physical feature is Adventure Isle, a moated double-island connected by two exciting bridges. Skilful

Pirate enthusiasts explore Captain Hook's ships

landscaping gives this area the impression of being larger than it really is. Elements from three well-known Disney movies are incorporated into the themes here: *Peter Pan, Treasure Island* and *Swiss Family Robinson*.

What to See in Adventureland

ADVENTURE ISLE ⭘⭘
The north section of Adventure Isle is given over to a pirate theme. The Jolly Roger flies by the lookout tower on Spyglass Hill. Below is Ben Gunn's Cave, with six different entrances: Dead Man's Maze, Davy Jones's Locker, and so on, leading to mysterious passages haunted by bats and skeletons. Waterfalls hurtle past gaps in the rock, shaped like an enormous skull. Captain Hook's Pirate Ship is moored in the cove nearby, and you can walk over the top deck to spy out the land. Down below, light snacks are served from the galley. At night Skull Rock and the waterfalls are illuminated. They look very eerie.

THE SWISS FAMILY ROBINSON TREEHOUSE ⭘⭘
Prominent on Adventure Isle is a strange-looking artificial banyan (fig) tree, rising 91ft (28m). In its branches, bearing 300,000 leaves and 50,000 flowers, is the ultimate treehouse, where the resourceful Robinson family have made a home from shipwrecked timbers. Wooden stairways lead to various rooms, while down by the roots of the tree is le Ventre de la Terre, where supplies from the wreck are stored behind bamboo bars. (The actual wreck can be seen under the suspended bridge.)

Walk the wobbly suspended bridge to Adventure Isle

Pirates Beach

© Disney

43

An exhilarating ride on Indiana Jones™ and the Temple of Peril: Backwards

INDIANA JONES™ AND THE TEMPLE OF PERIL: ✪✪✪ BACKWARDS

A daring high-speed roller coaster ride culminating in a thrilling loop the loop experience. We all know the fearless archaeologist whose adventures have been the subject of several exciting films. The setting here is an ancient temple full of hidden treasures, all in a wild, untamed jungle. Aboard a goldmine cart you begin a perilous chase up, over and under the mine site, past ancient statues and teetering columns. And if that isn't enough to get the adrenalin flowing, the ride is backwards all the way. This a popular ride so take advantage of the FASTPASS® (➤ 20).

ALADDIN'S ENCHANTED WORLD ✪✪

Situated in Adventureland Bazaar, this attraction brings to life the enchanted city of Aladdin's tales. As you walk through an Arabian Nights décor, various scenes from Aladdin appear before your eyes, with animated figures and special light and sound effects that help to carry you on the wings of your imagination from the city of Agrabah to the Cave of Wonders where the magic lamp lies hidden.

PIRATES OF THE CARIBBEAN ✪✪✪

One of the block-busting attractions of the Park, a must for everyone. There are similar attractions at the other Disney Theme Parks, too, but here the latest *Audio-Animatronics®*

44

technology is employed, giving an even wider range of special effects. As you make your way through the rocky grotto to the boats, you can hear roistering buccaneers singing their favourite song. You are about to embark on a time-travel adventure, going back to a 17th-century scene somewhere in the West Indies, where palms wave and the air is warm and balmy. The boat sets off through the moonlit Blue Lagoon and gradually the sounds of distant gunfire grow louder; a fortress is being shelled by a pirate ship. Pirates are attempting to scale the walls, daggers clutched between their teeth. The boat then passes inside the fortress. The ride is so packed with detailed scenery that it is hard to take everything in amid the general plunder and mayhem. Passengers can buy pirate souvenirs afterwards in Le Coffre du Capitaine.

As many as 124 *Audio-Animatronics*® figures are used, including animals. Some of the animated scenes are highly naturalistic and sophisticated: full of sword-fights, facial gestures and so on. The weapons are authentic replicas of 16th- and 17th-century pieces. The dialogue is mostly in colloquial French, but clues are almost entirely visual, so there is no great loss of enjoyment for non-French speakers. This ride is so action-packed that you could certainly do it more than once.

> **TIP**
>
> Do not let children eat too many sweets before they go on the rides.

You'll be amazed by the special effects at Pirates of the Caribbean

© Disney

© Disney

Fantasyland

©DISNEY

When you reach the neat gardens and fountains of Central Plaza, you can see straight ahead of you the mysterious gilded pinnacles of a truly fantastic castle, and the drawbridge is down, just waiting for you to cross. Sleeping Beauty Castle is the main landmark of Disneyland® Park. It is slap in the centre and unmissable, so it is always a good place to meet. As the spires can be seen from most sections of the Park, they can give bearings if you get lost.

If you approach Fantasyland from Central Plaza when the live show is on at the open-air Théâtre du Château at the foot of the castle, take time to watch as it will put you and your children in the right mood for the fairy-tale world you are about to enter. You would be surprised how many adults enjoy themselves watching Winnie the Pooh and Friends, Too!. These shows are renewed regularly but are always very popular. There is another live show in Fantasy Festival Stage, near Fantasyland Station. Most of Fantasyland's attractions are designed for younger guests; teenagers may find Dumbo the Flying Elephant a little beneath their dignity. At first, that is. The theme of Fantasyland, as its name suggests, is the world of fairytales: witches and dwarfs, princes and princesses, ginger-bread houses and magic wishing-wells. The European origin of these fairytales is heavily emphasised. Architecture ranges from quaint, Bavarian-looking cottages to the ambitious medieval whimsy of the castle itself.

Several of the attractions are similar in type: short rides through enclosed spaces, during which a fairy story is unfurled with many elaborate sets and moving figures. The characters are deliberately based on Disney animated films. There is no attempt to make them look like 'real people'. Queues for these attractions are lengthy. Pinocchio's Travels or Peter Pan's Flight are difficult to follow if you are not already familiar with the stories, though you can still enjoy the rides. Other attractions are of the fairground variety – in the form of classic merry-go-rounds and a few mild G-forces. If you know other Disney Theme Parks you will probably remember the block-busting and eternally popular 'it's a small world', here given more elaboration.

Alice's Curious Labyrinth

Completely new attractions are the hedge maze of Alice's Curious Labyrinth – again, a strongly European feature, and Fairytale Land.

Elsewhere in Fantasyland there are many shops selling toys and sweets, and there are also lots of fairytale eating places (designed mostly with children in mind), including one of the few restaurants in the Park with French cuisine, Auberge de Cendrillon. You can reach Fantasyland by the Disneyland® Railroad, but after that you must use your feet.

> ### TIP
>
> Catch the fantasy attractions when queues are short if you can – early or late in the day, or during meal-times and parades, when crowds will be thinner.

Pinocchio's Travels

TIP

Very young or
susceptible children
may find parts of
Snow White and the
Seven Dwarfs, The
Dragon's Lair and
Peter Pan's Flight
frightening.

What to See in Fantasyland

ALICE'S CURIOUS LABYRINTH ✪✪

Based, of course, on *Alice in Wonderland*, this maze of clipped yew and ivy hedges is 1,200ft (366m) long. The visitor passes characters and scenes from Alice: the Cheshire Cat, which rolls its eyes and twitches its tail, a blue caterpillar calmly smoking a hookah, strange birds and, of course, the choleric Queen of Hearts advocating decapitation at every turn. Eventually you reach a small purple castle, full of optical illusions. The jumping fountains transfix passers-by; arcs of water leap from pool to pool round the edge of the maze. The designs for some parts of this attraction are unusual and keep children amused for quite some time.

© Disney

*Children can lose
themselves for quite a
while in Alice's Curious
Labyrinth*

SNOW WHITE AND THE SEVEN DWARFS ✪
Climb aboard the diamond-mine cars outside the Dwarfs' cottage, and set off through this German fairytale, on which Walt Disney based one of his most successful animated films. The wicked queen does her stuff with the mirror and the poisoned apple, and Prince Charming appears at the end.

LANCELOT'S CAROUSEL ✪✪
A classic merry-go-round, with 86 ornate, medieval war horses trotting through fairytale scenes. An enjoyable, gentle ride.

CASEY JNR – LE PETIT TRAIN DU CIRCUS
Straight out of the Disney classic *Dumbo* this circus train rides up and down small hills and over bridges as it jerks its passengers swiftly round the miniature sets of Fairytale Land (▶51). A gentle ride that the whole family will enjoy.

DUMBO THE FLYING ELEPHANT ✪✪
The long queues for this ride testify to the popular appeal of this simple roundabout for young children. You can control the height at which your elephant flies.

Lancelot's Carousel, for those who like things a little more sedate

Dumbo the Flying Elephant, a star attraction

49

The Sleeping Beauty Castle

TIP

Check show times at Le Théâtre du Château or the Fantasy Festival Stage when you arrive.

'its a small world' – the world in miniature

SLEEPING BEAUTY CASTLE ✪✪✪

This is the archetypal interpretation of a castle – one we instantly recognise from the pages of any storybook, or from early Disney movies, such as the animated classic *Sleeping Beauty*. The design is based on illustrations from a 17th-century edition of *Les Très Riches Heures du Duc de Berry*, and the building rises 149ft (45.5m) above the moat. A technique known as 'forced perspective' has been employed, to give an illusion of even greater height. The pink walls are topped by 16 whimsical ornamental turrets of subtle, sea-blue tiles. Pennants, weather vanes and golden finials adorn the roofline; creepers hang from the walls; and enticing stairways lead to the central tower. Visitors can enter the castle by the drawbridge, or from the side by the wishing well (Le Puits Magique); don't forget to wish. Once inside, turn and look up at the front window – and wait a few seconds. Magically, its design will transform from two doves into a rose. This is a 'polage window', and it works by means of a rotating filter. Upstairs, in la Galerie de la Belle au Bois Dormant (Sleeping Beauty's Gallery) there is an exhibition of hand-woven Aubusson tapestries, colourful stained-glass windows made by English craftsmen and illuminated manuscripts depicting the famous story of *Sleeping Beauty*. From the balcony, the view over Fantasyland is splendid.

© Disney

"IT'S A SMALL WORLD" ✪✪✪

Like similar attractions at Tokyo, Orlando and Anaheim, this is a very popular and elaborate attraction. In Disneyland® Park it is a fantastic amalgam of many different architectural landmarks, ranging from Big Ben to the Leaning Tower of Pisa. The set is constructed in miniature. Every quarter of an hour a parade of animated figures troops around the base of the clocktower, and many exciting things happen before you are eventually told what time it is. Guests can a ride in canal boats past a gathering of *Audio-Animatronics®* 'children' from all parts of the globe. Norwegian figure-skaters give way to leprechauns, London's Beefeaters, Flamenco dancers, Balinese fan-dancers, and the like.

It is a saccharine show, but the technical effects are nonetheless impressive. There are nearly 280 different figures, representing a phenomenal effort by the Disney costume department.

MAD HATTER'S TEACUPS ✪✪

A pleasantly loony whirl in 18 giant teacups, placed on a roundabout, resulting in a bewildering pirouette of motion. You control the speed using a steering wheel.

STORYBOOK LAND ✪✪✪

Miniature scenes from European fairy tales unfold slowly as children of all ages take a canal cruise through familiar landscapes that re-create the magical appeal of delightful tales such as *Hansel and Gretel*, the *Little Mermaid* or *Beauty and the Beast*. But there is more...the imposing Mount Olympus where Greek gods once lived, Aladdin's cave and the legend of King Arthur.

Family fun on the Mad Hatter's Teacups

> **TIP**
> You may have an expensive time if you let your children investigate too many of the shops in Fantasyland.

TIP

Get a FASTPASS®
ticket for Peter Pan's
Flight as soon as you
arrive in Fantasyland.
It is a very popular
ride with extremely
long queues.

PETER PAN'S FLIGHT

Pirate galleons 'sail' over the rooftops of London to Never Land, giving an illusion of flight. A delightful journey for day-dreamers of all ages.

TWIRLING OLD MILL

An old windmill is the setting of this big wheel attraction that offers a good overall view of Fantasyland.

THE DRAGON LAIR

Chained by the neck in a dark cave of bubbling pools and stalactites is a leathery grey dragon, wonderfully terrifying. It makes gentle snorings and twitchings, then flashes its red eyes and gives fierce roars, smoke pouring from its nostrils. Its tail lashes in the water, while the wings move and claws tense. It is one of the most remarkable and sophisticated pieces of *Audio-Animatronics®* technology in the Disney Park. You can reach the lair from the mysterious shop called Merlin l'Enchanteur, carved into the rock of the castle.

PINOCCHIO'S TRAVELS

Based on the story told by Carlo Collodi. The cars pass from cheery Alpine landscapes into dangers and temptations, and then emerge back in Geppetto's shop, where the clockwork toys spring to life.

Pinocchio meets the crowds

© Disney

Discoveryland

This European version of Tomorrowland also looks back at the great inventors and visionaries of the past. Here, in France, Jules Verne is given a prominent role; H G Wells and Leonardo da Vinci are also featured.

©DISNEY

© Disney

Travel through time and space: science fiction, special effects and speed form the basis of the two shows (The Visionarium and Videopolis), and six attractions you will probably have to queue for: Star Tours, Autopia, Orbitron, The Mystery of the Nautilus, Honey, I Shrunk the Audience and Space Mountain.

If, as many people do, you tackle the Park clockwise, this is the last land you will come to, and psychologically it feels as though it should be. The architecture is futuristic, with lights and flashing lasers.

What to See in Discoveryland

AUTOPIA ✪

This is a popular attraction, consisting of a ride in a 'Car of the Future' through 'Solaria', a city of tomorrow. Your car is kept firmly on a specific track, and all you have to do is press the accelerator and steer.

> **TIP**
>
> You can steal a march on the queues by arriving early and walking from Main Street, U.S.A. to Discoveryland. Then head for popular attractions before everyone else arrives.

Try out your driving skills at Autopia

© Disney

53

HONEY, I SHRUNK THE AUDIENCE ✪✪✪

This original attraction, inspired by the two Disney success *Honey, I Shrunk the Kids* and *Honey, I Blew up the Kid*, opened to great acclaim in 1999. You watch as accident-prone inventor Wayne Szalinski (hero of the two films) demonstrates his shrinking and enlarging machine and commits his biggest blunder – pointing the machine at the audience! From the start you are carefully prepared for the worst as you are given special glasses to wear as you enter the first auditorium, where a multimedia pre-show whets the appetite. You are then ushered into the main auditorium and the action starts, as state of the art special effects create the highly convincing 'shrinking' effect, through 3D visual effects, surround-sound and touch sensations on leg and face. The show reaches its height when young Adam Szalinski picks up the auditorium and the whole theatre starts to shake…

THE MYSTERY OF THE NAUTILUS ✪✪✪

This attraction was inspired by Disney's movie *20,000 Leagues under the Sea* based on Jules Verne's novel. Docked in Discoveryland's lagoon, the Nautilus is Captain Nemo's submarine, the strange universe of an eccentric visionary who plays the organ at the bottom of the sea. An undersea passage, reached through a nearby lighthouse, leads to the interior of the submarine.

The tour of the vessel holds a few surprises in store for you as well as some spine-chilling sound and light effects. It begins in the Treasure Room and ends in the Engine Room.

Take to the sky on the Orbiton ride

© Disney

ORBITRON ✪✪

There is nothing new about the basic principle of this ride, but it certainly looks different. Bronze, copper and brass globes spin on various axes, the opposite way from the direction of your two-seater craft, so if you are at maximum height (controlled from inside) it seems quite fast. Queues can be very long, as there are only 12 passenger vehicles.

STAR TOURS ✪✪✪

This exciting attraction draws on the themes and special effects used in George Lucas's epic adventure, *Star Wars*.

© Disney

As much excitement is created by the build-up as by the ride itself. The sci-fi 'business' before you are actually strapped into your spacecraft, when visitors can watch friendly droids working, is all part of the fun, and certainly takes tedium out of queuing. The attraction is based on a popular comic theme: the novice driver. This one, unfortunately, is your pilot for the space flight. Fasten your seat-belts. The space craft pitches, rolls and jolts, while on-screen, rapidly moving images suggest you are falling or on some irrevocable collision course. Eventually, of course, you land safely to be greeted by Rox-N, a clever robot who presents the interactive computer games of L'Astroport Services Interstellaires (Star Tours Post-Show) in five languages. There is an X-ray detector with videoscreen projection to eliminate minute space creatures. There is also a sophisticated camera which takes your photograph and projects it on a large screen; you can then distort it at will by dragging your finger across the screen. But the most exciting game is Star Course when would-be pilots try their skill at avoiding obstacles while hurtling through space at high speed.

Prepare for lift-off at the Star Tours attraction

> ### TIP
> Get a FASTPASS® ticket for Star Tours. It is a very popular ride and can often have long queues.

TIP

If you feel like sitting down, time your meal at Café Hyperion during the Videopolis show.
Check the entertainment programme for times.

VIDEOPOLIS

The airship Hyperion marks this pavilion, which houses a large tiered auditorium, where visitors can enjoy videos relayed on four giant screens and regular live shows such as The Legend of the Lion King. The Café Hyperion offers a good view of the stage, so you can enjoy hamburgers and hotdogs while you watch. These are supported by unearthly special effects created by lasers, lights and artificial mist.

THE VISIONARIUM

This is an enjoyable production based on the time-travel theme, using the medium known as Circle-Vision 360®, which will be familiar to anyone who has visited the Disney Theme Parks in America. In these attractions the audience is completely surrounded by a belt of large cinema screens. The totality of this cinematic experience is achieved by using nine different cameras controlled by computer. Spectacular landscapes, many different perspectives and a very convincing illusion of movement are just some aspects of this entertaining show. In Disney's other Theme Parks, Circle-Vision films have been mostly confined to tourist travelogues, but here for the first time is a plot. There is a robot inventor called Time-keeper; 9-Eye, a robot with nine cameras around her head (for this creature is female, it seems); and Jules Verne as honorary guest, collected from the Paris Exposition of 1900 for a voyage through time. Gérard Depardieu puts in a brief appearance as an airport baggage handler and Jeremy Irons is HG Wells. The shooting of this film involved some adventures, including sending the expensive nine-camera turret under the sea.

SPACE MOUNTAIN – FROM THE EARTH TO THE MOON

This attraction undoubtedly marks the climax of a visit to the Disneyland® Park, for the setting, the sounds and the awe-inspiring darkness, torn by incandescent asteroids, are all designed to make you feel like pioneers embarking on a space adventure. The exhilarating experience begins long before boarding the rocket ship: while you slowly make your way through the heart of the impressive 118ft (36m) high 'mountain', you experience a taste

of the dangers ahead with meteorites and explosions all around. The curious but less daring may also enter the mountain and walk along gangways from which you get the most vivid impression of this fantastic space journey.But the count-down to blast off is ticking away and it is time for the rocket ship to enter the barrel of the 72ft- (22m) long Columbiad Cannon, inspired by Jules Verne's novel *From the Earth to the Moon* published in 1865, over 100 years before man first set foot on the moon. During the catapult launch, which lasts a mere 1.8 seconds, passengers experience an acceleration of 1.3g before plunging into space on a hair-raising half mile (1km) journey at a top speed of 43 miles (70km) per hour. In its efforts to avoid impending annihilation, the rocket ship makes three complete inversion loops while a sophisticated on-board audio system, synchronised with the ride experience, adds to the thrills, if that were still possible. Compared with other attractions of a similar type, Space Mountain represents a huge leap forward in innovation and technological precision, which enables a rocket ship to be launched every 36 seconds!

> ### TIP
> Be sure to get a FASTPASS® ticket for Space Mountain. It is probably the most popular ride in the Park and queues are almost always long.

A unique space adventure awaits at Space Mountain

© Disney

Food & Drink

Eating Disney-style is all part of the Disneyland® Resort Paris experience, and the choice is extensive. There are no food shops or restaurants within walking distance of the resort other than Disney ones, though picnic tables are provided near the Disneyland® Hotel for those who bring their own food. (Remember, you are not allowed to take food or drinks into the Parks.)

Eating Disney Style

Within the Disney Parks there are many different restaurants, serving a great range of international dishes, plus a range of *chariots gourmands* serving speciality foods, such as bagels and stir-fries, and a number of carts selling popcorn, ice-cream and beverages. In the resort's hotels there are a dozen or so thematic restaurants (also open to non-hotel residents; it is advisable to make a reservation). At Disney® Village, there are another half-dozen restaurants, plus a dinner-show venue. Many, but not all of the resort's restaurants stay open all day.

Dining at Agrabah Café Restaurant

Whichever Disney Park you are in you will find plenty of places to satisfy any sudden hunger pangs. Some restaurants have table service, at others you queue by counters, and some are no more than take-away snack bars. Child menus or child-size portions are served in table- or counter-service restaurants. Special diets, such as kosher, can also be catered for with advanced warning.

© Disney

Fast Food

At peak times the restaurants within the resort are geared to serve over 150,000 meals a day. Considering the speed and efficiency with which they do this, the quality is surprisingly high, and at least some notice is taken of many people's wish to eat healthier, less fat-laden diets. Inevitably, however, 'fast food' abounds, prepared daily in mass-catering quantities. Where else in France, though, could you dine on a palm-fringed Caribbean shore with boats sliding past your table, or munch spare ribs in a high-raftered Wild West barn full of wagon wheels and hay rakes?

Silver Spur Steakhouse, Frontièrland

Dinner at Disney's Sequoia Lodge®

What it Costs

Eating at the Disneyland® Resort Paris is not cheap, though some things are good value. If you are on a tight budget, avoid eating at the table-service restaurants. Stick to sensible, filling snacks from the *chariots gourmands*, such as beef and chicken kebabs in Adventureland or baked potatoes in Frontierland. Any of the counter-service restaurants will provide a satisfying plateful of food without breaking the bank if you feel like a sit-down meal, and all table-service restaurants provide a three-course set meal for rather less than the à la carte price. Credit cards are accepted and guests staying in the resort' can use their Disneyland® Resort Paris charge cards at most places in the Theme Parks—but remember it is cash only when using the food carts.

Background image © Disney

Walt Disney Studios® Park

Walt Disney Studios® Park, opened ten years after Disneyland® Park, is designed to take its guests to the very source of the Disney magic, on a thrilling interactive journey behind-the-scenes to discover some of the secrets of Disney animation, to marvel at special effects, to witness spectacular stunts and take part in a live television broadcast. And, anything can happen when Mickey takes over as cameraman! Lights on, take one!

The park is divided into four distinct production zones based on a real studio and includes ten attractions and several shops and restaurants. In addition, there is endless entertainment called 'Streetmosphere': actors, musicians and characters adding to the atmosphere of a real working film studio.

Loved by everyone, Chip and Dale

Front Lot

Beyond the Park's gates, the inviting courtyard shaded by palm trees with a fountain in its centre (could it be Mickey in disguise?!) reveals none of the excitement that lies ahead.

© Disney

The focal point of this area, known as 'Front Lot' in cinema jargon, is undoubtedly the 108ft-(33m) tall water tower topped by Mickey's famous pair of black ears. Originally used to fight fires, such towers became the symbol of a Hollywood film studio; this one was modelled on the water tower erected near the entrance to the Disney Studios in Burbank, California in 1939. And as you might expect, there is a definite 1930s air about the place. Beyond the courtyard lies the entrance to Disney Studio 1.

What to See on Front Lot

DISNEY STUDIO 1　　　　⭐⭐

Here you step straight into the glaring lights of a Hollywood film set, Hollywood Boulevard, packed with movie props and lined with shops and a restaurant, where guests become part of the action!

Studio 1 is a veiled reference to Walt Disney's studios in Los Angeles, which were the birthplace of the Mickey Mouse animated shorts and of Disney's first full-length animated film, Snow White and the Seven Dwarfs. Some of the sets are inspired by buildings that actually existed, others help to re-create the atmosphere of Hollywood during the first half of the 20th century.

© Disney

The famous water tower, a symbol of Disney Studios®

WALT DISNEY STUDIOS®
PARK IN FIGURES

- The park was designed by a team of 300 Imagineers
- It covers an area of 62 acres (25ha)
- Its construction required 5,000 tons of stainless steel, 1.5 million cubic ft of cement and 262 miles (421km) of radio cabling
- It prompted the creation of 1,500 direct and 3,000 indirect jobs
- The water tower, a symbol of Disney Studios, stands 108ft (33m) high

Backlot

According to studio jargon, this area is usually not on show...this is where the tricks of the trade are developed, perfected and eventually filmed, all very hush-hush and definitely out of bounds, but not at Walt Disney Studios® Park!

What to See on Backlot

© Disney

ARMAGEDDON, SPECIAL EFFECTS ✪✪✪

This attraction takes its name from the American science-fiction film featuring the Mir space station. The pre-show area pays tribute to the inventor of special effects, Frenchman George Méliès, and puts you in the mood for what is in store for you! Once you step on board the space station, the mounting suspense becomes almost unbearable as all sorts of apocalyptic things happen...or do they? Could it be that those visual and sound effects are more real than reality itself? Well the thrill is real enough anyway, so enjoy it!

ROCK'N'ROLLER COASTER STARRING AEROSMITH ✪✪✪

A spine-chilling ride with a difference! It has the speed, the acceleration, the loops, the turns, the drops that you'd expect...but it also has the music and stunning visual effects! Make use of the FASTPASS® ticket to reduce waiting time at this attraction (▶ 20).

MOTEURS ACTION STUNT SHOW SPECTACULAR ✪✪✪

This is what every James Bond fan would like to see...a live stunt show! And this is exactly what Walt Disney Studios® Park is offering you – a breathtaking spectacular staged up to five times a day in a 3,000-seat outdoor arena. The scene is a seaside village in southern France, the action: a live shooting of various stunts with purpose-designed powerful cars, motorbikes and jet skis and then you get a chance to see it all again...on screen!

Rock'n'roller Coaster

© Disney

See some amazing stunts performed at the Stunt Show Spectacular

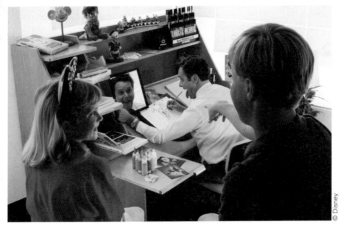

© Disney

Animation Courtyard

This is the temple of the art of animation for which the name of Disney became famous worldwide. Three attractions, including exhibits and shows, are devoted to the evolution of animation from its European origins to the most sophisticated feature-length animated pictures of our time.

Above/below: you won't believe your eyes at Art of Animation as sketches burst into life

What to See on Animation Courtyard

ART OF DISNEY ANIMATION ✪

© Disney

When he visited Disneyland® Resort Paris, before the opening of the new Park, Roy Disney, Walt Disney's nephew (at that time Chairman of Walt Disney Feature Animation), was thrilled by this attraction.

Creating the illusion of motion is a dream that goes back to prehistoric man. Many pioneers have tried to make this dream come true and the pre-show film pays homage to these now-forgotten forerunners. The pre-show area also displays various artefacts, some of them quite unique, such as the multi-plane camera developed by Walt Disney in the 1930s to add depth to animated images by allowing various parts of the same picture to be animated separately. And why not have a go yourself at the 'persistence of vision' apparatus?

The attraction itself, a sequence which takes place in three successive rooms, includes a film with highlights from Disney's animated classics that will whet your appetite for what follows in the second room, Drawn to Animation: a demonstration of how it is done by a Disney artist with the help of Mushu, the little red dragon from the film *Mulan*. After this, character animation will no longer hold any secret for you and you will be given a chance to try your newly acquired skill at the interactive play stations located in the last room.

© Disney

ANIMAGIQUE ✪✪
Staged in a 1,100-seat theatre, this 'black-light' show using giant fluorescent puppets, ultra-violet light and special effects is partly orchestrated by Donald Duck...with strange results as you can imagine! Characters from your favourite Disney animated pictures (Mickey, Donald, Pinocchio, the pink elephants, the whale...) come to life in this three-dimensional animated show...as if by magic!

FLYING CARPETS OVER AGRABAH ✪✪✪
Hang on to your magic carpet as you're whirled round a giant magic lamp and let your imagination take flight into a far-off land where illusion and reality become mixed up. It is advisable to make use of the FASTPASS® ticket on this very popular attraction.

Art of Animation

© Disney

It's like being in a real life movie at Catastophe Canyon

© Disney

Production Courtyard

A statue of Charlie Chaplin as he appeared in City Lights, one of his most moving films, marks the entrance to this part of Walt Disney Studios® Park. This is the hub of the studios, the place where it all happens, where the spectators' dream becomes reality... on screen!

© Disney

What to See on Production Courtyard

TELEVISION PRODUCTION TOUR ★

This is now home to the Disney Channel France and it is the very first time that a television network has been based inside a Disney Park! A tour guide shows guests round the Transmission Centre, from which Disney Channel programmes are broadcast throughout France, as well as round the Pre- and Post Production areas. Live broadcasts take place six days a week. Guests can watch the sequence of events from a glass corridor and get a real insight into the workings of a television studio. But that is not all...how about watching yourself appear on TV?

Disney Studio 1

© Disney

Production tour at Walt
Disney Television

CINÉMAGIQUE ✪✪

As the name implies, this show is a tribute to
the magic appeal of the European and US
cinema over the past hundred years. Featuring
a selection of the most exciting film excerpts
as well as a review of the actors and actresses
who are now part of the legend, it invites
guests to relive the cinema's greatest moments. Inside
the 1,100-seat theatre, do not be deceived by the 1930s
decor. The latest technology is here...you are about to
experience its powerful effects and witness a disconcerting but exciting fusion between fiction and reality!

STUDIO TRAM TOUR: BEHIND THE MAGIC ✪✪

If you think this is just a tourist ride round the production
area with a chance to see what goes on behind the
scenes....you're right....well not quite!

When you climb aboard the studio tram you will taken
on a fun-packed tour backstage. See film sets, props,
costumes and vehicles from some of your favourite
movies, and special effects that will no longer hold
secrets for you when you come out. But there is one
mighty detail that willl make all the difference to your flow
of adrenaline: your tram will take a dramatic detour via
Catastrophe Canyon and from then on it's all-hell-let-loose
as you find yourself at the heart of the special-effect
shooting of a series of hair-raising disasters! This is a
popular attraction.

Disney Movies

At Walt Disney Studios® Park get an insight into what goes on behind the scenes

© Disney

It is very likely that many of us have enjoyed watching at least one Walt Disney feature in our life. Kids will sit quietly transfixed in cinemas across the land as they gaze up at the screen where their favourite toon is brought to life courtesy of Uncle Walt.

In the early 1920s, Walt's first production studios were located in the back of a real estate office, where black-and-white cartoons like *Steamboat Willie* were conceived. Animals were easier than to humans to animate, and Mickey was ideal, drawn from a series of circles. In 1927 sound was added and colour followed a few years later.

Over the years the world has witnessed these simple treasures develop into feature length cartoon movies and computer generated masterpieces. There have been films about wild animals and their surroundings, live action movies starring human actors and those that combine both humans and cartoon characters. In more recent productions an all-star-cast has been used to provide the voices for the characters, including actor Tom Hanks who featured as Woody in *Toy Story*. Disney has won 32 Academy Awards for their films and for scientific contributions to filmmaking, and the original characters – Mickey Mouse, Donald Duck, Goofy and co. – have reached a legendary status in the present world of movie making. The folllowing is a potted history of most the Disney movies past and present.

The Movies

1923 *Alice Comedies* (with Ub Iwerks): 56 films mixing animation and live action.

1928 *Steamboat Willie*: first appearance of Mickey and Minnie Mouse, and the first animated film using synchronised sound. Only squeaks, sighs and whistles were recorded.

1929 '*Silly Symphonies*': 75 short animations in which plants and creatures come to life. The famous Skeleton Dance was the first of this series.

1930 *The Chain Gang*: first appearance of Pluto.

1932 *Flowers and Trees*: wins Disney's first Academy Award, and the first cartoon made in full colour. Mickey's Revue appears – also the first appearance of Goofy.

1934 *The Wise Little Hen*: Donald Duck first appears.

1937 *Snow White and the Seven Dwarfs*: the first full-length feature animation. Despite Roy Disney's gloomy predictions and the massive costs, a huge success.

1940 *Pinocchio* and *Fantasia* appear, denting the studio's budgets, but not its spirit.

1941 *Dumbo* wins an Academy Award for Best

Original Score.

1942 *Bambi* is premiered.

1943 *Der Führer's Face*: Donald Duck does his bit for the war effort, and the film wins an Academy Award. *Saludos Amigos* appears.

1950 *Treasure Island* and *Cinderella*: *Treasure Island* was a departure from Disney norms, using live actors.

1951 *Alice in Wonderland*

1953 *Peter Pan*

1954 *20,000 Leagues Under the Sea*: Academy Award for special effects.

1955 *Lady and the Tramp*

1959 *Sleeping Beauty*

1960 *Swiss Family Robinson*

1961 *One Hundred and One Dalmatians*

1964 *Mary Poppins*: six Academy Awards, including a Best Actress award for Julie Andrews.

1967 *The Jungle Book*

1970 *The Aristocats*

1973 *Robin Hood*

1977 *The Many Adventures of Winnie the Pooh*

1988 *Who Framed Roger Rabbit*: four Academy Awards, signalling Disney's return to success after many uncertain years following Walt's death.

1990 *The Little Mermaid*: two Academy Awards for musical content.

1991 *Beauty and the Beast*: two Academy Awards, and nomination as Best Picture.

1993 *Aladdin*

1994 *The Lion King*: the biggest box office success ever.

1995 *Pocahontas*

1995 *Toy Story 1*: the first fully animated movie to be produced using computer graphics.

1996 *The Hunchback of Notre-Dame*

1998 *Bug's Life*

1999 *Tarzan*

2001 *Atlantis*

2003 *Pirates of the Caribbean*: five Academy Awards; *Finding Nemo*: Academy Award for Best Animated Film; *Brother Bear*

Newest Releases

2004 *Haunted Mansion*; *Home on the Range*; *The Incredibles*; *Around the World in 80 Days*; *America's Heart & Soul*; *The Princess Diaries 2*

The Disney Cinema Parade, Walt Disney Studios®

Background image © Disney

Excursions

If your aim is to see a bit more of France during your visit to Disneyland® Resort Paris, there is plenty to do for all the family without having to travel too far. Shoppers will enthuse over the huge complex on the doorstep of Disneyland® Resort Paris at Val d' Europe and La Vallée Shopping Village, where you can find all the latest designer labels – many at reduced prices.

And of course, a short ride takes you into Paris with its fantastic array of smart shops, grand department stores and interesting markets, and where you can explore endless galleries, museums and famous sights. In the countryside around Disneyland® Resort Paris are several stunning chateaux, some very well known, such as Versailles and Fontainebleau, and other lesser-known little gems.

Colourful sculpture outside the Centre Georges Pompidou

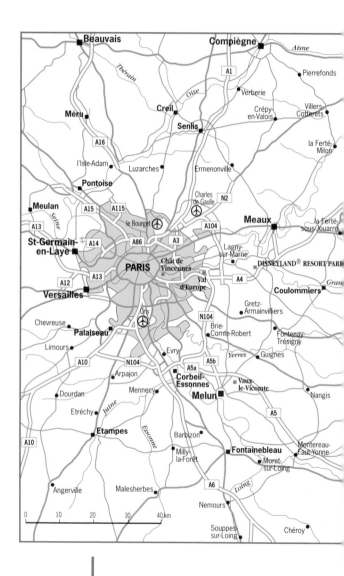

AROUND DISNEYLAND® RESORT PARIS

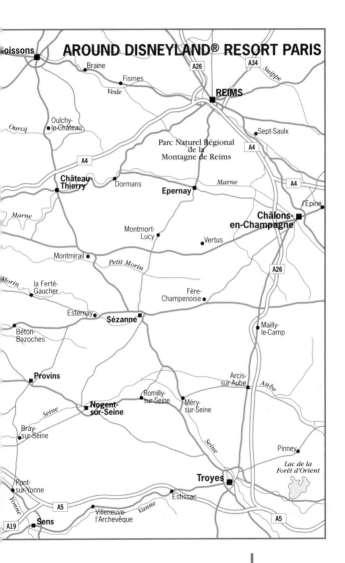

Soissons

Braine

Fismes

Vesle

A26

A34

Suippe

REIMS

Sept-Saulx

Oulchy-
le-Château

Ourcq

Parc Naturel Régional
de la
Montagne de Reims

A4

A4

A4

**Château-
Thierry**

Dormans

Epernay

Marne

l'Epine

**Châlons-
en-Champagne**

Marne

Montmort-
Lucy

Vertus

Montmirail

Petit Morin

A26

Morin

la Ferté-
Gaucher

Fère-
Champenoise

Esternay

Sézanne

Mailly-
le-Camp

Bèton-
Bazoches

Provins

Arcis-
sur-Aube

Aube

Romilly-
sur-Seine

**Nogent-
sur-Seine**

Méry-
sur-Seine

Seine

Bray-
sur-Seine

Pinney

*Lac de la
Forêt d'Orient*

Seine

Troyes

Pont-
sur-Yonne

A5

Estissac

Yonne

A19

Sens

Villeneuve-
l'Archevêque

Vanne

A5

There's always time to shop

© Disney

Val d'Europe

This purpose-built area is only 10 minutes drive from Disneyland® Resort Paris, exit 13 on the A4 motorway, and offers accommodation, shopping and places to eat, plus a Sea Life aquarium.

A new glass-and-metal complex offering shopping, eating and entertainment on a vast scale has recently sprung up close to Disneyland® Resort Paris. The International Shopping Centre on two levels includes a hypermarket and over 130 shops as well as La Vallée Outlet Shopping Village (► Where To Shop), a picturesque group of designer boutiques selling previous-season and end-of-line stock at discounted prices. Les Terrasses (nine restaurants and two bars offer a wide choice of menus with live music daily until midnight.

And there is more...**Aquarium Sea life Val d'Europe** and its 30 aquariums, displaying a fascinating marine world from jellyfish and eels to giant rays and sharks, invite you to journey down the River Seine to the Atlantic and across the ocean to the Caribbean. A fascinating experience as you walk through the 360° underwater glass tunnel. The colours of the exotic species of fish are stunning.

The European Sea life Network presents its own breeding programme for endangered seahorses and its campaign for shark conservation. Here you will find the largest collection of sharks in France and the exhibition 'Sharks, the True Story' opened in 2003. Further conservation projects include 'SOS' and 'Save Our Seas' and the aquarium works on joint projects with Greenpeace, WWF and the Whale and Dolphin Conservation Society.

LA VALLÉE®
OUTLET SHOPPING VILLAGE

Sea Life Val d' Europe
✉ Centre Commerical Val d'Europe, Espace 502, 14, Cours du Danube-Seris 77711, Marne-la-Vallée
☎ 01 60 42 33 66
🕐 Daily 10–5.30
🚇 RER A Val d' Europe
♿ Good
💷 Moderate
❓ Free parking, shop

SEA·LIFE
PARIS
Val d'Europe ★

Historic Châteaux

The Île de France, Paris's green belt, is well known for its splendid châteaux and great forests. An hour's drive southwards from Disneyland® Resort Paris will enable you to visit the architectural gems of Fontainebleu and Vaux-le-Vicomte and to explore one of the finest forests in the region. Just to the southwest of Paris is the huge chateau of Versailles, while on the eastern outskirts of Paris sits the formidable castle of Vicennes.

Below: *looking past neatly trimmed, conical-shaped trees, towards the Chateau de Fontainbleau*

FONTAINEBLEAU, CHÂTEAU DE ✪✪✪

The massive and beautiful château is the main draw, but the great hunting forest that surrounds the town provides a welcome retreat for Parisians. It is an excellent place for picnics, walking, cycling and riding, but is very busy at weekends. As the name suggests, a fountain or spring, now in the Jardin Anglais, is at the origin of this splendid royal residence, which started out as a hunting pavilion in the heart of the forest. The magnificent apartments of the château were transformed from medieval to Renaissance splendour by François I in the 16th century, and later kings also left their mark. The opulence of the decor is astonishing, especially the ceilings. The imposing horseshoe staircase decorating the main façade was the scene of Napoleon I's moving farewell to his faithful guard in 1814. In the grounds is the Etang des Carpes (carp pool) with a lovely pavilion at its centre and farther on the formal French gardens.

Fontainebleau – 39 miles (63km) south of Disneyland® Resort Paris
✉ 77300 Fontainebleau
☎ 01 60 71 50 70
🕐 Wed–Mon 9.30–5 (6 Jun–Sep). Closed 1 Jan, 1 May, 25 Dec
🍴 No café. Picnics allowed in the park but not gardens. Cafés and restaurants in the town (£–£££)
🚆 Gare de Lyon to Fontainebleau-Avon, then bus A or B
♿ Very good
💰 Moderate
❓ Guided tour, shops

Vaux-le-Vicomte – 28 miles
(45km) south of
Disneyland® Resort Paris

✉ Château de Vaux-le-
Vicomte, Domaine de
Vaux-le-Vicomte, 77950

☎ 01 64 14 41 90

🕐 Mid-Mar to mid-Nov
Mon–Fri 10–1, 2–6;
Sat–Sun 10–6

🍽 Cafeteria (£)

🚉 Gare de Lyon to Melun
then taxi

♿ None

💰 Expensive

🛒 Shops

*The Chateau de Vaux le
Vicomte is a masterpiece
of 17th-century French
architecture*

VAUX-LE-VICOMTE, CHÂTEAU DE ✪✪✪

Compared with Fontainebleau or Versailles, this château is small, but its moderate size seems only to enhance its attractiveness and means it can more easily be appreciated and enjoyed in a single visit. The interior contains many charming features and fine antiques, but the grounds are most impressive: illusory vistas, neat topiary, canals and terraced parterres shift before the eye like an Escher painting as you walk among them. In the stables is a museum (Musée des Equipages) devoted to horse-drawn carriages.

The château has an interesting story. It was built by the ambitious politician Nicolas Fouquet, in 1656: le Vau was the architect, Le Nôtre designed its lovely gardens, and Le Brun supervised the interior. After his gorgeous château was completed in 1661, Fouquet made what was to be the disastrous mistake of inviting Louis XIV to dinner, to impress him. The king was impressed, so impressed that he seethed with jealousy and fury at this parvenu. Fouquet was arrested on a trumped-up charge and his possessions were seized by the king, who commissioned the very same artists to upstage Vaux-le-Vicomte with an even more ambitious project – Versailles. As Fouquet languished in perpetual imprisonment, he must have reflected many times that those who sup with autocratic monarchs need a long spoon.

A fountain with gilded statues of Apollo rising out of the water on a horse-drawn trap in the gardens of the Château de Versailles

VERSAILLES, CHÂTEAU DE ✪✪✪

Versailles is the ultimate symbol of French grandeur, and the backdrop to the death of the monarchy. In 1661, when Louis XIV announced his intention of moving his court to this deserted swamp, it was to create a royal residence, seat of government and home to French nobility. Building continued until his death in 1715, by which time the 247-acre (100-ha) park had been tamed to perfection by landscape garden designer André Le Nôtre. Hundreds of statues, follies and fountains, and the royal retreats of the Grand and Petit Trianon relieve the formal symmetry, while rowing boats, bicycles and a minitrain now offer a diversion from history. The castle is huge (2,231ft/680m long) and it is impossible to see everything in the course of one visit. Aim for the first floor with the Grands Appartements (State Apartments), which include the staggeringly ornate Hall of Mirrors. The Petits Apartements display France's most priceless examples of 18th-century decoration and may be visited by guided tour only.

Versailles – 12 miles (20km) southwest of Paris
- ✉ Château de Versailles, 78000 Versailles
- ☎ 01 30 83 78 00
- 🕐 Chateau: Tue–Sun 9–5.30 (6.30 in summer) Parc: 7–5.30 (up to 9 depending season)
- 🍴 Café (£); restaurant (££)
- 🚉 Gare St-Lazare to Versailles Rive Droit
- ♿ Good
- 💷 Moderate
- ❓ Guided tours, shops

VINCENNES, CHÂTEAU DE ✪✪

This austere castle, situated on the easter outskirts of Paris, was a royal residence from the Middle Ages to the mid-17th century. Inside the defensive wall, there are in fact two castles: the 164ft (50m) high keep built in the 14th century; and the two classical pavilions (Le Pavilion du Reine and Le Pavilion du Roi) built by Le Vau for Cardinal Mazarin in 1652.

Vicennes – 4 miles (6km) east of Paris
- ✉ Château de Vicennes
- ☎ 01 48 08 31 20
- 🕐 Daily 10–noon, 1–5 (6 in summer). Closed 1 May, 1 Nov, 11 Nov, 25 Dec
- 🚇 Porte de Vincennes
- ♿ None 💷 Inexpensive
- ❓ Guided tours, shops

77

Paris

With so much to see in Paris, and if you are only making a short visit, it is worth deciding in advance what you really want to see. If it's views of the city you prefer head for the Eiffel Tower, the Pompidou Centre or Sacre Coeur. For art lovers there is the Louvre, the Musée D'Orsay and the Musée Rodin among a feast of museums. For spectacular churches seek out Notre Dame and the Sacre Coeur and for shoppers don't miss the area around Faubourg Saint-Honoré and the Champs-Elysées, while for a taste of old Paris take a boat trip down the River Seine.

CENTRE GEORGES POMPIDOU

More than a mere landmark in the extensive facelift that Paris has undergone since the 1970s, the high-tech Centre Pompidou (known to Parisians as Beaubourg) is a hive of changing cultural activity. Contemporary art, architecture, design, photography, theatre, cinema and dance are all represented, while the lofty structure itself offers exceptional views over central Paris. Take the transparent escalator tubes for a bird's-eye view of the piazza where jugglers, artists, musicians and portrait artists ply their trades to the teeming crowds.

✉ rue Rambuteau 75004
☎ 01 44 78 12 33
🕐 Wed–Mon 11–10. Museum and exhibits 11–9; Brancusi Workshop Mon–Fri 2–6; Library Mon, Wed–Fri noon–10, Sat, Sun 11–10
🍴 Restaurant (££); café (£); snack bar (£)
Ⓜ Rambuteau, Hôtel de Ville
🚌 38, 47, 75
🚆 RER Line A, B, Châtelet-Les Halles
♿ Excellent
💷 Permanent collections inexpensive; full ticket expensive
❓ Frequent lectures, concerts, parallel activities, Atelier des Enfants

View of the Arc de Triomphe from the Avenue des Champs Élysées

CHAMPS-ELYÉES/ARC DE TRIOMPHE

For most visitors this prestigious avenue epitomises French elegance, but it is also a dazzling place of entertainment and a luxury shopping mall. These days the Champs Élysées may be dominated by car showrooms, but plush cinemas, classy shops and one or two fashionable watering holes still remain to tempt those who want to see and be seen. The Arc de Triomphe is an image of French national pride, built as a symbol of Napoleon's military strength. There is a wonderful view from the top, 164ft (50m) above street level.

✉ Champs Élysées 75008
🍴 Choice of restaurants (£–£££)
Ⓜ Charles de Gaulle-Étoile, Georges V, Franklin D Roosevelt, Champs-Élysées-Clémenceau
🚌 32, 42, 73
❓ It can take around 30 minutes to walk from the Arc de Triomphe to place de la Concorde

JARDIN DU LUXEMBOURG

If you want to get away from the bustle during your trip to Paris these gardens are serene in all weathers and are the epitome of French landscaping. Natural attractions include shady chestnuts, potted orange and palm trees, lawns and even an experimental fruit garden and orchard, while fountains, tennis courts, beehives, a puppet theatre and children's playgrounds offer other distractions. Joggers circumnavigate the gardens, while sunbathers and bookworms settle into the park chairs. Statues of the queens of France, artists and writers are dotted about the terraces and avenues.

✉ 15 rue de Vaugirard 75006 (various entries around the park)
🕐 Daily 7.30AM–9.30PM, Apr–Oct; 8.15–5, rest of year (times may vary)
🍴 Open-air cafés, kiosk restaurant (£–££)
Ⓜ Odéon
🚇 RER Luxembourg
🚌 21, 27, 38, 58, 82, 84, 85, 89
♿ Very good
🎟 Free

LES MARAIS

The sedate old-world atmosphere of this historic enclave at the heart of the city, its architectural beauty and its cultural diversity are unique. Extending from the Hôtel de Ville to the place de la Bastille on the Right Bank of the Seine, it offers visitors narrow picturesque streets, cafés and bistros, elegant mansions, tiny boutiques and a lively population. Across on the Left Bank you will find the **Latin Quarter**, a trendy student district.

✉ Les Marais
Ⓜ Hôtel de Ville
🚌 29, 75

✉ Quartier Latin
Ⓜ Cluny-La Sorbonne

MUSÉE DU LOUVRE

The world's largest museum was originally a medieval castle. It first took shape as an art gallery under François I, eager to display his Italian loot. The vast collection of some 30,000 exhibits is arranged on four floors of three wings, while beneath the elegant Cour Carrée (courtyard) lie the keep and dungeons of the original medieval fortress. Almost 5,000 years of art are covered, starting with Egyptian antiquities and culminating with European painting up to 1848.

✉ 99 rue de Rivoli 75001
☎ 01 40 20 53 17; recorded information 01 40 20 51 51
🕐 Thu–Sun 9–6, Mon and Wed 9AM–9.45PM
🍴 Wide selection of restaurants and cafés (£–££)
Ⓜ Palais-Royal, Musée du Louvre
🚌 21, 27, 39, 48, 67, 68, 69, 72, 75, 76, 81, 95
♿ Excellent
🎟 Moderate until 3PM, inexpensive after 3pm and Sun; free first Sun of every month
❓ Guided tours and audioguides

Inside Musée Du Louvre

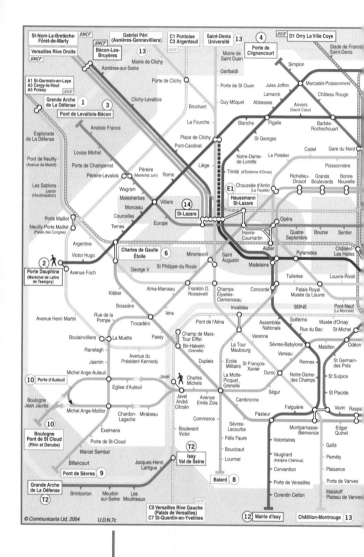

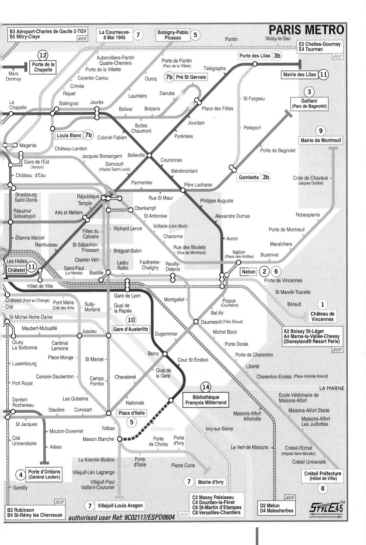

⊠ Monmartre, 75018 Paris
Ⓜ Abbesses, Lamarck-
Caulaincourt
🚌 Montmartrobus

Sacré Coeur
⊠ place du Parvis du Sacré
Coeur, 75018
☎ 01 53 41 89 00;
🕐 Basilica daily
7AM–11PM; dome and
crypt 9–6 (also until 7 in
summer)
Ⓜ Abbesses (from here,
walk along rue Yvonne Le
Tac, then take funicular or
walk up steps)
🚌 30, 54, 80, 85
Montmartrobus
♿ Very good
🎫 Basilica free; dome and
crypt inexpensive

Notre-Dame
⊠ place du Parvis Notre-
Dame 75004
☎ 01 42 34 56 10; crypt 01
43 29 83 51;
🕐 Cathedral Mon–Fri
8–6.45; closed on some
religious feast days.
Tower daily 9.30–7.30,
Apr–Sep (also until 11PM,
Sat–Sun, Jul–Aug);
10–5.30, rest of year.
Treasure Mon– Sat
9.30–11.30, 1–5.30
Ⓜ Cité, St-Michel
🚌 24, 47
🚇 RER Lines B and C,
St-Michel
♿ Good (but not in towers)
🎫 Cathedral free; tower
inexpensive; treasure
inexpensive

Above: *Sacre Coeur*
Right: *Notre Dame*

Tower Eiffel
⊠ Champ de Mars 75007
☎ 01 44 11 23 23;
🕐 Daily 9.30AM–11AM
(stairs 9.30–6.30),
Sep–Jun; 9AM–midnight,
Jul–Aug (last admission
one hour before closing)
🍴 Restaurants (£–£££)
Ⓜ Bir-Hakeim 42, 69, 72,
82, 87
🚇 RER Line C, Tour Eiffel
♿ Very good (to 2nd floor)
🎫 Expensive; stairs
inexpensive

82

MONTMARTRE/SACRÉ COEUR

Once the haunt of famous artists, Montmartre retains something of a village atmosphere and the area has become a major tourist attraction. At the top of the village is the basilica of Sacré Coeur, an unmistakable feature of the Paris skyline that magnetises the crowds arriving either by funicular or via the steep steps of the terraced garden. The view of Paris is breathtaking, stretching for 31 miles (50km) around the city. The dome is the second-highest point in Paris after the Eiffel Tower.

NOTRE-DAME/RIVER SEINE

Notre Dame is a masterpiece of Gothic architecture and one of Paris's most famous landmarks with its 295-ft (90m) spire and world-renowned flying buttresses. You can admire it if you take a boat trip along the Seine. There are many splendid monuments to see along the river banks in particular on the Île Saint-Louis and the Ile de la Cité, the historic centre of Paris.

TOUR EIFFEL

Paris's most famous landmark has been towering above the city for more than a hundred years, yet its universal appeal remains constant. When built for the World Exhibition in 1899 by Gustave Eiffel its 984ft (300m) height made it the tallest building in the world and an unprecedented technological achievement. Its iron frame weighs 7,000 tonnes and 40 tonnes of paint are used to repaint it every seven years. There are three levels, all accessible by lift or stairs – a breathtaking 1,710 steps to the top. The genius of the construction by Eiffel shows in the fact that the tower sways no more than 5cm in high winds. It remained the world's highest structure for more than 40 years. Eiffel kept his office here until his death in 1923.

© Disney

Where To...

Above: *take a relaxing swim at a hotel indoor swimming pool*

Disneyland® Park

Dinner Shows
No matter what time of year you visit Disneyland® Resort Paris there will always be an exciting themed dinner show to go to. Whether it's Christmas or New Year, or a themed Disney character evening there's fun for all the family.

Tips
Try to choose off-peak mealtimes to minimise queuing. The best times to eat lunch are before midday, or after 2PM. Miss the 8–9PM evening rush if you can. If you have already seen the parades, choose to eat when they are on, as the restaurants are likely to be much emptier.

If the Park restaurants seem too busy, simply walk through the gates to Disney® Village, where you will have a choice of another half-dozen eating places, which are probably less busy at lunchtime. Or alternatively, a picnic area is located between Guest Parking and the Parks entrance.

At busy times when the Parks are crowded, you can make a same-day reservation at any table-service restaurant. Or you can call the Reservation Service, who will reserve a table in the restaurant of your choice at any of the Disney® Hotels, in the Parks or in Disney® Village. Information about this service is available at the Conciergerie of Disney® Hotels and Selected Hotels, in the Parks or in the restaurant where you want to eat. Don't worry if you can't get into your first choice; there are plenty of options. The last thing you need worry about here is starving!

Opening Times
During certain periods some restaurants may be closed but most stay open all the time the Parks are in full swing. Some in Disney® Village open only in the evening and keep going until well after midnight. Most hotel restaurants serve dinner until 11PM at least. If you have your heart set on a particular place to eat it is best to check the opening hours first

Main Street, U.S.A.

Bagel cart
You may spot this in Central Plaza, toasting bagels and adding your choice of toppings. It is just one of many food carts (*chariots gourmands*) selling a variety of snacks and refreshments in the Park.

Cable Car Bake Shop
Lots of wicked things most of us should not be eating are on offer in this agreeable (if dark) setting. There is booth seating, decorated with sepia photos of San Franciscan streetcars.

Casey's Corner
Head here if you are a baseball freak. Hot dogs and chips are available. Eat them beside bats and balls and Coke logos, and beneath Tiffany lamps. You may be regaled with ragtime music.

The Coffee Grinder
Just follow your nose to the tempting aroma and make your choice of fresh coffee.

Cookie Kitchen
A parting-shot temptation as you try to resist the Cable Car Bake Shop. This counter sells muffins, brownies and, of course, cookies.

Gibson Girl Ice Cream Parlour
Milkshakes, sundaes, banana

splits and fruity ice-creams are all here in a pink- and-white candy-striped environment, with girls in frilly dresses and straw boaters.

The Ice Cream Company

Why not treat yourself and sample your favourite flavour in a cornet topped with an array of tasty toppings.

Market House Deli

An old-fashioned general store in the best Disney tradition. Sausages hang from the ceiling, and casks and lovely old tins deck the dresser shelves. There is also an ancient cast-iron stove and an old weighing machine. While admiring the décor, you can munch American sandwiches, such as hot pastrami on rye, and sample turkey and tuna salad.

Plaza Gardens Restaurant

A spacious building beside the Sleeping Beauty Castle. With an outdoor patio, this is a good place to sit and watch the world, or the parades, go by. The sparkling 19th-century Victorian-style interior is full of columns, statues, stained-glass domes and mirrors. A wide choice of self-service fare consists of salads, hot dishes like Maryland crab cakes, and a luscious array of desserts (included in the price of a main course).

Victoria's Home-Style Cooking

Cosy domestic interiors from the 1890s set the tone for this counter-service. Eat Victoria's delicious 'pot pies' by the harmonium, or in the

conservatory, perhaps watching a passing parade. Mouth-watering deserts to die for.

Walt's – An American Restaurant

Dedicated to the life and work of Walt Disney, this is one of the smartest restaurants in the Park. The two-storey building offers elegant table service in nine intimate little dining-rooms, all based on different themes. Take a table inside, or on the outside patio. For good views of the parades, bag an (expensive) table upstairs near the window. Classy American food, including Veal Oscar, rack of lamb with goat's cheese, crab cakes and baked, stuffed Maine lobster. A cheaper and simpler menu is offered downstairs and on the patio.

Frontierland

Cowboy Cookout Barbecue

Tap your feet to country music at this large barn that houses a Wild-Western-style barbecue, with inside and outside seating for large numbers. The rustic theme includes agricultural implements, harnesses, quilts, wagon wheels, butter churns and so on, in a hay-loft/grain silo setting.

Fuente del Oro Restaurant

Tex-Mex specials are all here: counter-service tacos, chilli con carne and fajitas. The building is an attractive New Mexican one in adobe style, with a courtyard where you can eat while being regaled by the Mariachis, a Mexican group.

Party Time

For something different children can celebrate their birthdays Disney-style. The party takes place in Plaza Gardens in Disneyland® Park where Disney characters help with the celebrations with a birthday buffet, complete with cake and a surprise present. But even if there is no birthday to celebrate you can still take tea with Disney characters.

No Alcohol Policy

Disneyland® Park, like its cousins in Florida, California and Tokyo, was meant to be rigidly alcohol-free. The Theme Parks' priority 'guests' are children, and in such an environment adult pleasures (or vices) were thought to have no place. At first, Walt's strict dictum prevailed even in France, where children grow up accustomed to a watered glass of wine. However, faced with much derision and amazement from the host country the iron Disney rule was eventually bent.

Last Chance Café

Last stop before the Haunted Manor. Counter service for sandwiches, turkey drumsticks and beverages. It is carefully styled as a bandit hideout.

Lucky Nugget Saloon

This western style bar houses a dance show that is shown several times a day and is also a counter-service restaurant. The menu features many favourite American dishes including spare ribs.

Silver Spur Steakhouse

The smart folks of Thunder Mesa dine here, in stylish 19th-century surroundings, and (needless to say) prime rib steak, cooked the way you like it, is the speciality of the house; the chicken breasts and Mexican specialities are also good.

Adventureland

Blue Lagoon Restaurant

This is located at the entrance of Pirates of the Caribbean, and diners have a view of boats slipping past on their voyage of discovery. The scene – a Caribbean night, lit by torches, with tropical vegetation all around – make this a delightful place to eat. Caribbean specialities and fish predominate: snapper, swordfish and other delicacies wrapped in banana leaves. As it is very popular, it is worth booking in advance if you want a table at a busy time.

Café del la Brousse

A snack bar with thatched huts on a terrace overlooking Adventure Isle, and a most pleasant place to sit. Sadly, the interesting-sounding North African specialities that were to be sold here have been replaced by hot dogs (albeit spicy ones) and chips, due to the patrons' lack of enthusiasm for anything exotic. Can this really be gastronomic France? Open summer only.

Captain Hook's Gallery

Sandwiches and cakes are available in this galleon anchored off Skull Rock, which is the haunt of pirates.

Colonel Hathi's Pizza Outpost

Tucked away in the bamboo forest, this makes a pleasant retreat. Built in colonial Victorian style, this counter-service restaurant contains mementos of many exciting explorations: native masks, a plane propeller, safari gear, hunting trophies and photographs. You can choose to sit on the veranda, or inside – a central sunken dining area contains a great tropical tree where animated macaws and toucans perch; the Charter Room is a stone-built, cosier room with a fireplace.

Restaurant Agrabah Café

Situated at the entrance to Adventureland from Central Plaza, this counter-service restaurant offers a three-course exotic buffet including paella, moussaka, curried lamb, spicy chicken, and other treats, all served with rice and mixed vegetables.

Restaurant Hakuna Matata

A counter-service restaurant in an African hut with ethnic

animal ceramics, baskets and carvings. Lamb curry and Moroccan meatballs are staples, plus Mickey's fun meal (for children).

Fantasyland

Auberge de Cendrillon
Cinderella's country inn is the smartest restaurant in Fantasyland, with beams and a cosy fireplace. Look out for Cinderella's pumpkin carriage in an alcove. Hosts and hostesses wear 17th and 18th-century costumes, in keeping with the elegant Louis XIV and XV furnishings. The restaurant serves traditional French cuisine and the menu changes regularly. As it is usually very busy during peak times it is best to book.

Le Chalet de la Marionette
This is Pinocchio's favourite restaurant! Fairytale frescos and Tyrolean charm smother this large counter-service restaurant. Chicken and chips and cheeseburgers, followed by apple strudel, are examples of the sort of fare it offers regularly.

Fantasia Gelati
Italian ice-creams can be consumed outside on the patio. As its adjacent to the parade route, it tends to fill up at parade times and immediately afterwards so queues can be extensive.

March Hare Refreshments
Stop off at this strange little cottage for drinks, cookies and brownies. Bright tables are set outside for a tea party.

The Old Mill
In the style of an old Dutch windmill. Snacks of all kinds such as pannini, fritters and fruit tarts, plus soft drinks and frozen yoghurt are on sale. Ideal for tea and biscuits or a hot chocolate after dark.

Pizzeria Bella Notte
Italianate façades set the tone for a feast of pizza and pasta in a setting of hams and garlic. There is also a Bacchic theme of grapes and wine casks.

Toad Hall Restaurant
The expansive Mr Toad invites guests to partake of fish and chips wrapped in newspaper, and roast beef sandwiches at his fine Elizabethan home. The interior is full of *Wind in the Willows* characters.

Discoveryland

Buzz Lightyear's Pizza Planet Restaurant
This pizzeria is conveniently situated close to one of the best attractions in Discoveryland – Honey, I Shrunk the Audience. There is also a children's play area.

Café Hyperion
The Jules Verne airship, Hyperion, is suspended above the entrance to Videopolis. Inside, this fast counter-service restaurant offers salads, burgers and Italian fast food to carry into the auditorium to sustain you through the show.

Chariots Gourmands
A sausage cart (grilled sausages on bread with onions) and a doughnut cart produce the fastest food in Discoveryland.

Just a Little Tipple
Alcohol is now served in four of Disneyland® Park's restaurants: Walt's – an American Restaurant (Main Street U.S.A.), the Auberge de Cendrillon (Fantasyland), the Blue Lagoon Restaurant (Adventureland), and the Silver Spur Steakhouse (Frontierland). Of course, the Disney® Village restaurants and all the hotels serve alcohol.

Elsewhere at Disneyland® Resort Paris

Themed Foods

When choosing your Disneyland® Resort Paris hotel you might well consider the type of food each hotel serves. Each has a theme to its food as well. If meat's your thing try the hearty American grills and barbeques at Disney's Davy Crockett Ranch®, Disney's Hotel Cheyenne® and Disney's Sequoia Lodge®. For seafood lovers there's Disney's Newport Bay Club® and at the Disneyland® Hotel there's excellent California cuisine. The atmosphere of the New York clubs is re-created in Disney's New York Hotel® where the food is refined and the service slick and at Disney's Sante Fe Hotel® you'll find European specialities and Tex-Mex dishes.

Walt Disney Studios®

There are 12 themed kiosks and trucks spread around the Park selling light meals such as hot dogs, pizzas, salads, quiches and chicken wings. Also sandwiches, ice-cream, pastries, popcorn and beverages, which guests can enjoy while sitting at the open terrace.

Backlot Express Restaurant

A counter-service restaurant with a relaxed backstage feel. Club and baguette sandwiches, quiches, salads and pastries.

Rendez-vous des Stars

Undoubtedly the place to be seen! This art-deco-style, buffet-service restaurant serves international and European cuisine.

Restaurant en Coulisse

This counter-service restaurant on two floors, with pizzas, hamburgers, chicken, salads and ice-cream on the menu, forms part of the glamorous decor of Hollywood Boulevard in Disney Studio 1.

Disney Hotels

Disney's Davy Crockett Ranch®
Crockett's Tavern

An attractive log-cabin restaurant, serving American home-style cooking for breakfast (and lunch in peak season) and dinner.

Disneyland® Hotel
California Grill

This elegant dining room has an open kitchen, where you can see Californian specialities being prepared. Lovely view over Main Street, U.S.A.

Café Fantasia

A pretty café furnished in pink with a muscial theme incorporated in its decor.

Disney's Hotel Cheyenne®
Chuckwagon Café

Guests and visitors eat at the Chuckwagon Cafe, a free-flow marketplace along Texan lines, where harnesses and bales of hay deck the high-raftered restaurant.

Disney's Hotel New York®
Manhattan Restaurant

This slick and smart restaurant is a 1930s experience redolent of cocktails and dinner-dances and Big Band music, with fine dining in luxurious surroundings. When you've finsihed eating retire to the Manhattan Lounge, a perfect venue for aperitifs or after-dinner drinks,

Parkside Diner

Eat food from Brooklyn, Chinatown and Fifth Avenyue in a New York atmosphere. A good place to enjoy an evening drink or a casual (but chic) meal.

Disney's Hotel Santa Fe®
La Cantina

An imaginative Tex-Mex desert café, with petrol pumps and pick-up trucks among the food-stalls. An excellent place to take breakfast).

Disney's Newport Bay Club®
Yacht Club
This speciality seafood restaurant invites you on a gourmet cruise in nautical-style surroundings.

Cape Cod
From the Cape Cod restaurant guests overlook a flashing lighthouse by the shores of Lake Disney®, where boats bob in summer.

Disney's Sequoia Lodge®
Hunter's Grill
You'll find hearty grills and spit-roasts at the Hunter's Grill.

Beaver® Creek Tavern
A good place for a relaxing family meals. International cuisine in an authentic American National Park environment.

Disneyland® Resort Paris Selected Hotels

Holiday Inn
L'Etoile
With good views of the Vallée du Grand Morin, this restaurant serves international and traditional French cuisine. There is a terrace for summer dining.
☎ 01 64 63 37 37

My Travel Explorers Hotel
The Captain's Library
Table service with a smile. The menu features cuisine from around the world.
Marco's Pizza Parlour
Marco's offers lunchtime Italian specialities and takeaways.
☎ 01 60 42 60 60

Kyriad Hotel
Hotel Restaurant
Decorated in the local style of the Brie region, this restaurant serves traditonal French cooking.
☎ 01 60 43 61 61

Mövenpick Dream Castle
Musketeer's
Fun family restaurant offering sumptuous buffets with a selection of international dishes.
Sanssouci
Dine on a variety of dishes in an 18th-century rococo setting.
☎ 01 64 17 90 00

Disney® Village

Annette's Diner
This is a typical 1950s-style diner serving giant burgers, sundaes and milkshakes. Join in with the shoobi-doo and hum to the classic music from the likes of Elvis and Chuck Berry, while waitresses on roller-skates dash up and down and jump on tables amd dance to 'Grease Lightning'.

Billy Bob's Country Western Saloon
Shine up your cowboy boots and come on down to this Nashville saloon that resounds with country-and-western music. Enjoy a fixed-price Texas-style buffet with wine or beer.

Café Mickey
Come here to meet your favourite Disney characters. Overlooking Lake Disney®, this two-storey restaurant and cocktail bar offers Californian specialities, such as rosemary honey pork

Vegetarian Options?
With so much emphasis on big American dishes such as grills, hamburgers and hot dogs and the French love of meat dishes too, this may not seem the best place for non-meat eaters. You will have to be selective and chose the vegetarian pizzas, salads and sandwich options. If you eat fish, try the great fish dishes at the Blue Lagoon Restaurant in Adventureland. And don't forget the ice cream – the choice is amazing.

Character Dining

To be sure of getting the full Disney experience start the day with a huge American breakfast accompanied by Disney characters. This is the perfect opportunity to meet them, get autographs, have your photo taken with your favourites and, above all, spend more time getting to know Mickey himself. Character Breakfasts are held at Café Mickey in Disney® Village and Walt's – An American Restaurant on Main Street, U.S.A in Disneyland® Park. It is best to book well in advance.

spare ribs and a good selection of wines. Don't miss the amazing all-you-can-eat dessert buffet.

King Ludwig's Castle

This large restaurant on two levels is confined within the ramparts of an authentic castle. At King Ludwig's you can see the history that inspired Walt to create his Sleeping Beauty Castle. The menu offers Bavarian specialities, such as *weiner schnitzel* and braised mushrooms with *spätzles* or cream sauce, and you can easily imagine you're dining in Munich as you sample pretzels in the Octoberfest tradition. Sumptuous desserts include Black Forest cake and strudel. The beer is from a reputable Bavarian brewery. Nice outside terrace.

Les Snacks

Feeling peckish between meals? Disney® Village has a wide variety of snacks to offer with counter service. Try the hot dogs or jacket potatoes.

McDonald's

This fast food chain offers no surprises but the Commedia dell'Arte decor is original, and there is a large indoor play area based on the theme of Leonardo da Vinci's discoveries. Located by the Disney® Village marina.

Planet Hollywood®

A spherical restaurant at the entrance of Disney® Village serving Californian cuisine in a movie decor. Look for the famous handprints and memorabilia from well-known movies and their

stars. And why not try some of the great cocktails?

Rainforest Café

The building looks like a mud hut, an appropriate style for the equatorial rainforest, and the restaurant is dedicated to the protection of animals. Here you can eat exotic dishes surrounded by wild animals and giant aquariums. Gift shop.

New York Style Sandwiches

An authentic New York deli where giant pickle jars and elaborate speciality bread form the window display. Hot pastrami on rye, cream cheese on a bagel, or a classic bologna could precede Manhattan spice cake. You get substantial side dishes of potato salad or coleslaw.

Sports Bar

Watch a non-stop round of televised sport on numerous TV monitors while munching on hot dogs and sandwiches.

The Steakhouse

Prime rib and T-bones are served in a building evoking a Chicago meat-packing warehouse. Classic wines (many Californian), and good desserts, such as brownies and cheesecakes, are sold.

Wild West Dinner

Treat the family to a traditional Wild West meal with all the trimmings. While you eat your cowboy dinner, which includes chicken, roast potatoes and ribs, you can watch Buffalo Bill's Wild West Show. There's plenty of action with horses, a buffalo chase and stagecoach hold-ups.

Excursions

Fontainebleau
🚉 Gare de Lyon to Fontainebleau-Avon then 🚌 A or B

L'Atrium (£–££)
Pizzeria in the town centre; with attractive year-round terrace dining.
✉ 20 rue France, 77300 Fontainebleau ☎ 01 64 22 18 36
🕐 Lunch, dinner

Le Montijo (££)
Brasserie in a luxury hotel facing the château; terrace in summer.
✉ Grand Hôtel de l'Aigle Noir, 27 place Napoléon Bonaparte, 77300 Fontainebleau ☎ 01 60 74 60 00 🕐 Lunch, dinner

Le Caveau des Ducs (££)
Elegant restaurant in vaulted cellars; terrace in summer.
✉ 24 rue Ferrare, 77300 Fontainebleau ☎ 01 64 22 05 05
🕐 Lunch, dinner

Around the Forêt de Fontainebleau

Barbizon
L'Angélus (££)
Convivial gastronomic restaurant with a terrace in summer.
✉ 31 rue Grande, 77630 Barbizon ☎ 01 60 66 44 30
🕐 Lunch, dinner; closed Tue

Hostellerie du Bas-Préau (££)
Haute cuisine meals served in the garden. Queen Elizabeth II and Emperor Hiro Hito have both stayed here.
✉ 22 rue Grande, 77630 Barbizon ☎ 01 60 66 40 05
🕐 Lunch, dinner

Bourron-Marlotte
Les Prémices (££)
Within the Fontainebleau forest; it is possible to eat on the ouside terrace in summer.
✉ 12 bis rue Blaise de Montsquou, 77780 Burron-Marlotte ☎ 01 64 78 33 00
🕐 Lunch, dinner; closed Sun dinner, Mon and first two weeks in Aug

Vaux-le-Vicomte
🚉 Gare de Lyon to Melun

La Mare au Diable (££)
Lovely old house with beams 16 miles (10km) from Vaux-le-Vicomte; terrace for summer meals.
✉ RN6, 77550 Melun-Sénart ☎ 01 64 10 20 90 🕐 Lunch, dinner; closed Sun dinner, Mon

Versailles
🚉 Gare St-Lazare to Versailles Rive-Droite; RER C to Versailles Rive Gauche

Le Boeuf à la Mode (£)
Old-fashioned brasserie with sunny terrace serving excellent duck and vegetable spaghettis.
✉ 4 rue au Pain, 78000 Versailles ☎ 01 39 50 31 99
🕐 Lunch, dinner

La Cuisine Bourgeoise (££)
Tasty refined cuisine served in cosy surroundings; all perfect on a day out to Versailles.
✉ 10 boulevard du Roi, 78000 Versailles ☎ 01 39 53 11 38
🕐 Lunch, dinner; closed Sat lunch, Sun, Mon and 3 weeks in Aug

Le Potager du Roy (£–££)
Very good-value bistro in elegant surroundings.
✉ 1 rue du Maréchal-Joffre, 78000 Versailles ☎ 01 39 50 35 34 🕐 Lunch, dinner; closed Sun dinner and Mon

Prices
Prices for a three-course meal vary from around €11 to over €152; the average price for each restaurant listed is shown by the pound symbol:
£   = up to €23
££   = €23–€80
£££ = over €80

The same price rating as for Paris has been applied to restaurants in nearby towns; however, you can expect to get much better value for money outside the capital; it is also important to remember that service finishes earlier in the evening than in Paris, usually around 9:30.

Paris

Value for Money

Whenever possible, choose one of the fixed menus rather than à la carte. Also note that menus are less expensive at lunchtime and that, unless otherwise specified, service is included in the prices quoted. Wines are generally expensive but house wines are often worth trying and are more reasonably priced. Restaurants usually serve meals from midday to 2PM and from 7.30 to 10.30PM. Brasseries (the word means breweries) are restaurants where one can often eat at any time of the day. Bistros are usually more modest (although some of them are very fashionable) and convivial, boasting quick friendly service.

L'Alsace (££)

Alsatian specialities and seafood; terrace in summer.
✉ 39 avenue des Champs-Elysées, 75008 ☎ 01 53 93 97 00 🕐 24 hours Ⓜ Franklin-D Roosevelt

Blue Elephant (££)

Thai cuisine in an appropriate setting near Bastille. Try the *chiang rai*.
✉ 43 rue de la Roquette, 75011 ☎ 01 47 00 42 00 🕐 Lunch, dinner; closed Sat lunch Ⓜ Voltaire

Bistro Romain (£–££)

One of 12 Bistro Romain restaurants in Paris. This one, in the Champs-Elysées, has an opulent setting but food is basic pasta and plenty of it. Some dishes, including the chocolate mousse, is on an 'as much as you can eat' basis.
✉ 26 avenue des Champs-Elysées, 75008 ☎ 01 53 75 17 84 🕐 Daily 11.30AM–1AM Ⓜ Franklin-D Roosevelt

Boulangerie Paul (£)

Have a coffee, tea or hot chocolate at this attractively decorated bakery and try one of their delicious pastries. Also all sorts of specialised breads, from multi-grains to bacon bread.
✉ 77 rue de Seine, 75006 ☎ 01 55 42 02 23 🕐 Daily 7:30AM–8PM Ⓜ Odéon

Chez Madame Vong (£)

Chinese and Vietnamese cuisine from Canton.
✉ 10 rue de la Grande Truanderie, 75001 ☎ 01 42 97 49 07 🕐 Lunch, dinner; closed Sat and Sun lunch Ⓜ Les Halles

Le Ciel de Paris (££–£££)

On the 56th floor of the Tour Montparnasse and said to be the highest restaurant in Europe. Enjoy the views while you eat.
✉ Tour Montparnasse, 33 avenue du Maine, 75015 ☎ 01 40 64 77 64 🕐 Lunch, dinner Ⓜ Montparnasse-Bienvenüe

Coffee Parisien (£)

An interesting combination – a Parisian bistro serving American diner-style food located in Saint Germain-des-Prés. Nice for Sunday brunch. Check out the cheeseburgers.
✉ 4 rue Princesse,75006 ☎ 01 43 54 18 18 🕐 Daily noon–midnight Ⓜ Mabillon, St-Germain-des-Prés

Coté Seine (£–££)

Attractively situated along the embankment between Notre-Dame and the Pont Neuf. Very good value for money; booking advisable.
✉ 45 quai des Grands-Augustins, 75006 ☎ 01 43 54 49 73 🕐 Dinner only Ⓜ St-Michel

La Coupole (££)

Famous brasserie from the 1920s with art deco setting and excellent seafood. Reasonable late-night menu (after 11PM).
✉ 102 boulevard du Montparnasse, 75014 ☎ 01 43 20 14 20 🕐 Daily 8:30AM–1AM Ⓜ Vavin

Findi (££)

Among elegant clientele you might catch sight of a celebrity at this restaurant serving traditional Italian cuisine in a modern setting, Food includes Parma ham and homemade pasta. Also a delicatessen.
✉ 24 avenue George V, off

Champs Élysées, 75008 ☎ 01 47 20 14 78 🕐 Lunch, dinner 🚇 George V

Le Fouquet (££)
Try this popular Parisian institution on the Champs Élysées, an excellent spot for people-watching. A snack menu can be found in the bar or on the terrace.
✉ 99 avenue des Champs-Élysées, 75008 ☎ 01 47 23 70 60 🕐 Lunch, dinner 🚇 George V

Hard Rock Café (£–££)
Relaxed atmosphere and plenty of buzz for eating hamburgers, grills and steaks.
✉ 14 boulevard Montmartre, 75009 ☎ 01 53 24 60 00 🕐 Daily noon–2am 🚇 Grands-Boulevards

Hippopotamus (£–££)
With nearly 20 outlets of this chain restaurant in Paris you can be sure of a good grill and salad in a child-friendly environment. Good prices.
✉ 1 boulevard Beaumarchais, 75004 ☎ 01 44 61 90 40 🕐 Daily 8AM–12.30AM 🚇 Bastille

Le Vieux Bistro (£–££)
Facing the north side of Notre Dame; traditional French cooking includes *boeuf bourguignon* (beef stew).
✉ 14 rue deu Cloitre, Note Dame, 75004 ☎ 0143 54 18 95 🕐 Lunch, dinner 🚇 Cité

Lucas Carton (£££)
Haute cuisine in an authentic late 19th-century building with decor by Pajorelle. Try the roast duck with honey and spices or the delicious saddle of lamb.
✉ 9 place de Madeleine, 75008 ☎ 0142 65 22 90 🕐 Lunch, dinner; closed Sat lunch, Sun 🚇 Madeleine

Nos Ancêtres les Gaulois (££)
Convivial atmosphere; menu includes as much wine as you can drink
✉ 39 rue St-Louis-en-l'Ile, 75004 ☎ 01 46 33 66 07 🕐 Dinner only, lunch on Sun 🚇 Pont-Marie

Le Paradis du Fruit (££)
Chain restaurant for vegetarians with excellent salads and delicious fresh fruit. This branch has delightful views of the Seine.
✉ 29 quai des Grand Augustins, 75006 ☎ 01 43 54 51 42 🕐 Lunch, dinner 🚇 Montparnasse-Bienvenüe

Piccolo Teatro (£)
Refreshing and inspired vegetarian dishes. Try the excellent soups.
✉ 6 rue des Ecouffes, 75004 ☎ 01 42 72 17 79 🕐 Lunch, dinner; closed Mon, Christmas 🚇 St-Paul

Terminus Nord (££)
A 1920s-style brasserie near the Gard du Nord; the speciality is duck's *foie gras* with apple and raisins and also seafood.
✉ 23 rue de Dunkerque, 75010 ☎ 01 42 85 05 15 🕐 Lunch, dinner 🚇 Garie du Nord

Train Bleu (££)
Brasserie with late 19th-century décor illustrating the journey from Paris to the Mediterranean.
✉ Place Louis Armand, Gare de Lyon, 75012 ☎ 01 43 43 09 06 🕐 Lunch, dinner 🚇 Gare de Lyon

Fast Food and Brunch
When the first McDonald's opened in Paris, most people thought it would be a flop! Instead, fast food has become part of the French way of life and now the mecca of gastronomy is about to adopt another Anglo-Saxon habit – the brunch. More and more bistros in central Paris now specialise in this 'new' kind of meal, definitely 'in'. In addition to McDonald's, popular fast food eateries and cafés include Flunch, Pat à Pain, Quick and Columbus Café. Popular chains include Bistro Romain, Buffalo Grill, Chez Clément, Courtepaille, El Rancho, Hippopotamus, Indiana Café and Pizza Hut. All serve children's menus and are reasonably priced.

Staying in the Magic

Hotels are open all year round but hotel rates fluctuate according to season, so check all reservation details first with your travel agent or with Disneyland® Resort Paris Reservations (▶ 107) for telephone numbers and Internet address).

Privileges

If you stay at one of the seven Disneyland® Resort Paris themed hotels you can enjoy certain privileges denied to other visitors, such as guaranteed access to the Disney Parks (which may close to other visitors on severely crowded days). Free shuttle buses to and from your hotel are provided (except Disneyland® Hotel and Disney's Davy Crocket Ranch®).

Disneyland® Hotel

This rambling pink confection is one of the most striking landmarks of Disneyland® Resort Paris. In terms of bedrooms it is the smallest of the hotels, though you would never think so to look at it. Its florid, Victorian-style gables and turrets, topped with pointed white finials, triumphantly straddle the entrance gates to Disneyland® Park. From Main Street, U.S.A., just inside the turnstiles, it is as noticeable as the castle, and many rooms have views of the Disney Park. The hotel seems utterly confident of its status as the flagship, and it is easily the most Disneyesque of all the buildings in the resort area. Designed by the architects of Disney 'Imagineering', it evokes the grand seaside palaces that graced the smart resorts of Florida and California at the turn of the 20th century. This is very much a family hotel, with thematic references to Disney cartoon characters. Features include a huge reception lobby with chandeliers dripping with ivy leaves, and a promenade, where a piano is played in an elegant lounge. The two restaurants and themed café offer a variety of lavish fare. The most luxurious hotel in the resort, finding your way around its complex layout takes some time. The hotel also offers Castle Club VIP service with luxurious suites, a private lounge where breakfast is available and soft drinks are served all day, and other additional privileges for an extra charge.
☎ 01 60 45 65 00

Disney's Hotel New York®

If you have seen Florida's Walt Disney World Resort you will instantly recognise the post-modernist handiwork of the celebrated American architect Michael Graves. His fantasy hotels in Orlando have a similarly extravagant style. Disney's Hotel New York® re-creates the landscapes of the Big Apple in a subtle palette of warm terracotta, dove grey and soft salmon. Inside, every last feature of the hotel, down to the Empire State Building lampstands in the bedrooms, echoes the theme. The effect is sophisticated, but fun. It is a more adult environment than the Disneyland® Hotel, and this hotel hosts Disney's lucrative sideline, the convention business (a very large conference centre is attached). Rooms overlook paved plazas or shady gardens and tennis courts. Though it's in the same category, Disney's Hotel New York® is slightly less expensive than the Disneyland® Hotel.
☎ 01 60 45 73 00
🚌 free shuttle

Disney's Newport Bay Club®

The irregular, creamy clapboard architecture with the grey-green roofs conjures up a tang of salt spray and a whiff of ozone. This is New England, the Atlantic seaboard. The New York architect Robert Stern designed this elaborate whimsy with classical touches, reminiscent of the Yacht and Beach Clubs at Walt Disney World Resort in Florida. Inside, the atmosphere is elegantly restful in shades of blue and grey. Bedrooms and corridors continue the nautical theme, with porthole windows and ship's tiller headboards. Enjoy an apéritif at the Captain's Quarters Bar or relax in the Fisherman's Wharf lounge. The hotel has its own convention centre.

☎ 01 60 45 55 00
🚌 free shuttle

Disney's Sequoia Lodge®

Embryonic redwood forests surround the timber wings and shallow, copper-green rooftops of this hotel, bent on re-creating the atmosphere of an American National Park lodge. Decor consists of lots of redwood veneer and grey stone. The main feature of the bar area is a huge, stone-faced fireplace, where there are real log fires. The imaginative swimming pool has waterslides and hot springs, and is one of this hotel's most attractive points. Bedrooms are decorated with wooden furniture and patchwork quilts.

☎ 01 60 45 51 00
🚌 free shuttle

Disney's Hotel Cheyenne®

A taste of the Old Wild West. Here you will find a life-size stage set of High Noon, where covered wagons stand in the streets, and you check in at the Town Bank by the Hangman's Tree. You could be sleeping in any one of 14 separate, wood-framed buildings. The Red Garter Saloon is the place for a drink, but do not expect a peaceful time here. It is very much geared to families, and

the atmosphere is cheerfully gregarious. The bedrooms are all cowboy-style, while Fort Apache, in the grounds, is a new style of adventure playground.

☎ 01 60 45 62 00
🚌 free shuttle

Disney's Hotel Santa Fe®

We are somewhere in New Mexico at this hotel, marked by a large 'drive-in cinema screen' sign bearing the likeness of Clint Eastwood. A complex of blocks encapsulating the atmosphere of the desert lies behind it, with colours ranging from blues and violets to earth tones. Between the blocks are mysterious sculpted objects, a flying saucer, a volcano, rusting automobiles and giant cacti. The theories behind the architecture of this hotel are complex, and it is worth following the various 'trails' between the buildings that architect Antoine Predock created (the Trail of Legends, the Trail of Infinite Space, and so on). Bedrooms are tastefully designed, using Pueblo Indian themes.

☎ 016045 78 007
🚌 free shuttle

Disney's Davy Crockett Ranch®

Self-catering cabins. The ranch is about 15 minutes drive from the Disney Parks and Disney Village, south of the A4, so be prepared to use your car on a regular basis since there is no bus service available. However, parking at the Disney Parks is free to guests of Disney's Davy Crockett Ranch®. An extensive 140-acre (57ha)

Location

All the Disney Hotels (apart from Disney's Davy Crockett Ranch®) are within walking distance of the entrance gates to the Disneyland® Resort Paris Theme Parks, though to make life even easier a fleet of buses whirls round the resort at frequent intervals, taking visitors to the bus station, less than five minutes' walk from the turnstiles. The seven existing hotels all lie quite close together, around the artificial stretches of water christened Lake Disney® and Rio Grande.

Themed Hotels

The Disney Hotels' architecture is a subject in itself. Several world-renowned architects have created them, and the ways in which themes have been encapsulated are startling and innovative – each a separate mini-Disney Park in itself – from the sophistication of Manhattan to the seclusion of the national parks, the pioneer spirit of the Wild West and the lazy southern atmosphere of a New Mexico village. All are highly theatrical, endeavouring to give their guests a variety of thematic experiences. If you want a total Disney experience, you should stay at the Resort.

patch of mature oak and beech woodland allows visitors to sample an outdoor experience in pioneer style. The luxurious trailer-home cabins have microwave oven, telephone, toaster, dishwasher and a large colour TV, and a maid service every other day. Breakfast is included and can be eaten in Crockett's Tavern or collected and taken back to your cabin. Other features include a small farm of domestic animals, sports facilities (tennis, volleyball, basketball, pétanque), and a swimming pool with waterfalls, bridges, whirlpools, slides and water cannon, housed in a huge, light and airy log cabin. Bicycles or electric golf carts can be hired to ride round the site. An on-site shop provides a wide range of groceries and toiletries, films, sweets and toys.

☎ 01 60 45 69 00

Selected Hotels

Holiday Inn

French country manor-style, hotel set in a 10-acre (4ha) park with a lake and views across the Grand Morin Valley. This friendly, family hotel was opened in June 2003 and is just 10 minutes from the park gates. A circus theme focuses throughout. The modern family rooms have contemporary artwork on the walls and a children's area with bunks, TV and video games. Restaurant; bar; indoor pool; fitness club; children's play area.

✉ 20 avenue de la Fosse des Pressoirs, Marne la Vallée, Val de France ☎ 01-64 63 37 37; 0800 905 999 (reservations)

📺 free shuttle

Kyriad Hotel

Built in 2003 and styled on a traditional farm from the Brie region, overlooking woodland. All rooms are air-conditioned, can sleep up to 4 people and have TV. A free bus runs to the Disney Park gates (about 5 miles/3km) and to the RER stations. Restaurant and two bars.

✉ 10 avenue de la Fosse des Pressoirs, Marne la Vallée, Val de France ☎ 01 60 43 61 61

📺 free shuttle

MyTravel's Explorer Hotel

The two-star rating belies the quality of this family hotel, opened in spring 2003, based on a pirate-cum-nautical theme. The family bedrooms can accommodate 4–10 people and have TV video games. There are two restaurants, plus a pizza takeaway and three bars. Large indoor swimming pool; children's play area.

✉ 50 avenue de la Fosse des Pressoirs, Marne la Vallée, Val de France ☎ 01 60 42 60 00

📺 free shuttle

Movenpick Dream Castle

You can live like a king at this imaginary castle, opened in 2004.only 10 minutes from the Park gates. Family orientated, the rooms have one king size bed and bunks, and are equipped with all modern facilties. Some have lake views. There's lots for the children – playground, splash and fun pool and fairytale storytelling –while the adults enjoy the fitness room and spa. Two restaurants and terrace eating in summer.

✉ 40 avenue de la Fosse des Pressoirs, Marne la Vallée, Val de France ☎ 01 64 17 90 11

📺 free shuttle

Staying Near the Magic

Acostel
Less expensive, independent small hotel with great character and charm.
✉ 336 avenue de la Victoire (R.N.3), Meaux ☎ 01 64 33 28 58

Auberge du Cheval Blanc
This small hotel of 22 rooms built in the 18th century offers a taste of old France. Only five minutes drive from the Disney Parks. Lounge/bar and restaurant.
✉ 2 rue de Lagny, Jossigny ☎ 01 64 02 24 27

Auberge de Gonfalon
A quiet stylish hotel by the River Marne that offers luxury in a peaceful setting, and has most facilities. Slightly farther from Disneyland® Resort Paris than other hotels listed here.
✉ 2 rue de l'Englise, Germiny l'Evêque ☎ 01 64 33 16 05

Campanile
Motel-style chain hotel with 97 rooms that projects a warm friendly atmosphere, five minutes walk from the RER metro and 6 miles (12km) from Disneyland® Resort Paris. Good sized rooms and a pleasant restaurant.
✉ 8 rue Marie Curie, ZAC du centre Ville, Bussy-St-Georges ☎ 01 64 66 62 62 🚇 Metro RER Line A (15 min)

Demeure de la Catounière
Small good-value hotel with a good restaurant. Pool and tennis, and golf nearby.
✉ 1 rue de l'Englise, Sancy-les Meaux ☎ 01 60 25 71 74

Golf Hôtel
Near Disneyland® Resort Paris (about 6 miles/12km) set in peaceful countryside.

The many activities include a swimming pool, table tennis, indoor and outdoor play area, and access to an 18-hole golf course. Restaurant serving French cuisine.
✉ 15 avenue du Golf, Bussy-St-Georges ☎ 01 64 66 30 30 📱 free shuttle to RER 🚇 Metro RER Line A (15 min)

Hôtel du Moulin de Paris
Comfortable, friendly hotel with 82 rooms, 2 miles (3km) from the Disney Parks and within walking distance of Disney® Village; so guests can fully appreciate the nightlife. The family-sized rooms have TV and internet service. Fitness room and sauna; restaurant.
✉ 60 rue du Moulin a Vent, Magny-la-Hongre ☎ 01 60 43 77 77 📱 free shuttle to Disney Parks (9AM-11AM and 8PM-10PM)

Hôtel l'Elysee Val d'Europe
Located at the Val d'Europe International Shopping Centre, only 2 miles (3km) from the Disney Parks, with the RER metro just across the street. A family hotel of excellent quality, modern in decor but still delightful with its authentic Parisian architecture. Good restaurant.
✉ 7 Cours de Danube. Val de Europe ☎ 01 64 63 33 33 🚇 RER Line A (5 min) to the Parks

Kyriad Hotel, Esbly
Swiss chalet-style hotel in the charming village of Esbly (about 4 miles (6km) from Disneyland® Resort Paris) and great value for money. All the ensuite rooms have TV and tea and coffee making facilities. Restaurant.
✉ 12 Av Charles de Gaulle, Esbly ☎ 01 64 17 10 10

Chain Motels
Numerous box-like motels are springing up around Marne-la-Vallée to cater for the new influx of visitors. Many of these belong to chains such as Campanile, Mercure, Ibis, Novotel or Kyriad. Do not expect anything very fancy or interesting; these are purely intended to provide practical, adequate accommodation for brief stopovers. Most of the big chains produce brochures, with useful location plans. Many are in charmless locations on busy roads and suffer from traffic noise; a few are handily placed for the RER stations on the Marne-le-Vallée line, but you generally need a car. Most motels provide some sort of restaurant, where the food, if not exacly haute cuisine, is authentically French and less expensive than in Disneyland® Resort Paris.

Family-run Hotels

The countryside immediately around Disneyland® Resort Paris is of little interest. If you have notions of staying in some quaint country *auberge* within a few minutes' drive of the resort, dispel them now. Most accommodation that serves the Disneyland® Resort Paris area of Marne-la-Vallée is modern, consisting of box-like motels or business hotels. Although, if you prefer small, privately run family hotels, there are a few a bit further afield; get the local Logis de France list. The Île-de-France Maison du Tourisme (opposite Disney® Village) produces a useful list of local accommodation and is very helpful about where to stay. It will make your reservation for a small fee.

Mercure, Lognes

Charming, simple hotel with a touch of quality in a quite green location. The 85 rooms are newly renovated, have satellite TV, internet access and a mini bar. Other facilities include a restaurant, sauna, fitness room and outside play area. About 9 miles (15km) from Disneyland® Resort Paris and 15 minutes from the RER metro.

✉ **Boulevard du Mandinet, Lognes** ☎ **01 64 80 02 50**
🚇 **Metro RER Line A**

Mercure, Noisy-le-Grand

Well positioned with easy access to both Disney Parks (11 miles/18km) and Paris, and close to the RER and motorways. The 192 luxury air-conditioned rooms have internet access and satellite TV. Other facilities include a swimming pool, sauna and restaurant.

✉ **Boulevard du Levant, Noisy-le-Grand** ☎ **33 489 88 40 05**
🚇 **Métro RER Line A (20 min)**

Novotel Atria

Modern hotel with good levels of comfort and standards. Located mid-way between Disneyland® Resort Paris and Paris itself, close to the motorway leading direct to the Parks (11 miles/18kms) and a short walk from the RER métro station. The 144 rooms are fully equipped with all modern facilities. Restaurant and swimming pool.

✉ **2 allee Bienvenue, Noisy-le-Grand** ☎ **01 48 15 60 60?**
🚇 **Métro RER Line A (20 min)**

Novotel Marne-la-Vallée

Modern, good-value hotel that opens onto a flowery central terrace and outdoor swimming pool. There are 197 air-conditioned rooms with well-fitted bathrooms. About 7 miles (12km) from Disneyland® Resort Paris.

✉ **Collégien** ☎ **01 64 80 53 53**

La Pierre Tourneville, Esbly

Budget hotel belonging to the Hotel Akena chain, convenient for the Disney Parks; only five minutes by car.

✉ **77450 Isles-les-Villenoy, Esbly** ☎ **01 60 04 42 42**

Saphir Hotel

Modern building set in lovely gardens. In a small town with direct access to the motorway and 15–20 minutes drive to Disneyland® Resort Paris. The 180 large bedrooms are tastefully decorated and well-equipped. Suites are available. A leisure complex has an indoor heated pool, plus sauna, gym, billard room, and tennis court. Restaurant.

✉ **Aire des Bercheres, Pontault Combault** ☎ **33 4 89 88 40 05**
🚇 **Métro RER Line A (20 min)**

Tulip Hotel

This elegant hotel with a startling white façade is in the heart of Bussy Saint Georges, 656ft (200m) from the railway station and 5 minutes drive from Disneyland® Resort Paris. The 87 smart bedrooms are comfortable and well equipped and the Pizza & Pasta restaurant serves traditional French and Italian cuisine.

✉ **44 boulevard Antonie Giroust, Bussy Saint Georges** ☎ **01 64 66 11 11** 🚇 **Métro RER Line A (15 minutes)**

Excursions

Fontainebleau
🚉 Gare de Lyon to Fontainebleau-Avon

Grand Hôtel de l'Aigle Noir (£££)
Napoleon III-style decoration is prominent at this hotel facing the castle; fitness club, indoor swimming pool and very good restaurant.
✉ 27 place Napoléon Bonaparte, 77300 Fontainebleau ☎ 01 60 74 60 00

Hôtel Le Richelieu (£)
Reasonably priced yet comfortable hotel, one of the Logis de France traditional establishments.
✉ 4 rue Richelieu, 77300 Fontainebleau ☎ 01 64 22 26 46

Around the Forêt de Fontainebleau

Barbizon
Hôtel Les Charmettes (£)
Picturesque timber-framed Logis de France hotel. Amenities include a restaurant, a bar. and garden terrace.
✉ 40 Grande-Rue, 77630 Barbizon ☎ 01 60 66 40 21

Hostellerie de la Clé d'Or (£)
A former coaching-inn with bedrooms overlooking the peaceful garden. There is an attractive terrace for summer meals.
✉ 73 Grande-Rue, 77630 Barbizon ☎ 01 60 66 40 96

Hôtel Les Pléiades (£)
A former painter's house turned into a hotel in the 'painters' village! Splendid terrace for summer meals. The hotel is noted for its refined cuisine.
✉ 21 Grande-Rue, 77630 Barbizon ☎ 01 60 66 40 25

Versailles
🚉 Gare St-Lazare to Versailles Rive Droite; RER C to Versailles Rive Gauche

Relais de Courlande (£)
Attractive converted 16th-century farmhouse; hydrotherapy facilities.
✉ 23 rue de la Division Leclerc, 78350 Les Loges-en-Josas ☎ 01 30 83 84 00

Sofitel Château de Versailles (£££)
Luxury château hotel next to Château de Versailles.
✉ 2bis avenue de Paris, 78000 Versailles ☎ 01 39 07 46 46

Trianon Palace (£££)
This luxury establishment, on the edge of the Parc de Versailles, boasts an exclusive fitness club, two tennis courts and golf and riding facilities.
✉ 1 boulevard de la Reine, 78000 Versailles ☎ 01 30 84 50 00

Saint-Germain-en-Laye (just north of Versailles)
🚉 RER Saint-Germain-en-Laye

Hôtel Cazaudehore-La Forestière (££)
Relaxation is the keynote in this large hotel.
✉ 1 avenue du Président Kennedy, 78100 Saint-Germain-en-Laye ☎ Hotel: 01 39 10 38 38, restaurant: 01 30 61 64 64

Hôtel Ermitage des Loges (££)
There's music on Wednesday and Thursday nights in the hotel bar; excellent restaurant.
✉ 11 avenue des Loges, 78100 Saint-Germain-en-Laye ☎ 01 39 21 50 90

Staying Away
You can visit all the excursions mentioned in this book on a day-out basis but you may fancy staying a night or two away from the resort either in Paris or somewhere more secluded. Or if you are touring France by car and just wish to visit Disneyland® Resort Paris for a day or two you might also choose to stay elsewhere. If you decide to make Paris your base it is quite easy to travel each day to the resort.

Paris

Prices

Prices indicated below are per double room:

£ = up to €100
££ = €100–€200
£££ = over €200

Note that luxury hotels such as the Ritz can charge over €700 for a double room. Payment can be made by credit card in most hotels except in some budget hotels.

Staying Near the Action

There is little point in choosing to stay in one of Paris's nondescript easterly suburbs, thinking you will be that much nearer Disneyland® Resort Paris. You will miss out both on the excitement of Disneyland® Resort Paris and the bright lights of Paris. There are obviously vast numbers of hotels to choose from in all areas and a range of price levels. You may prefer a small independent hotel or to choose from one of the well-known chains such as Best Western, Comfort, Mecure or Ibis for example, all of which have several hotels in Paris. The journey by Metro from the centre of Paris to the resort on RER line A4 takes about 40 minutes.

Hôtel de l'Abbaye (£££)

A roaring log fire and a delightful inner garden ensure comfort whatever the season.

✉ 10 rue Cassette, 75006
☎ 01 45 44 38 11; www.hotel-abbaye.com 🚇 St-Sulpice

Hôtel d'Angleterre Saint-Germain-des-Prés (££–£££)

The largest rooms of this quiet luxury Holiday Inn hotel overlook the secluded garden.

✉ 44 rue Jacob, 75006
☎ 01 42 60 34 72;
www.holidayinn.com
🚇 St-Germain-des-Prés

Hôtel du Bois (££)

Situated in a smart district 656ft (200m) from the Arc de Triomphe and Champs-Elysée, this hotel has small but elegant bedrooms decorated in warm soft tones.

✉ 11 rue du Dôme, 75016
☎ 01 45 00 31 96; www.hoteldubois.com 🚇 Kléber, Charles de Gaulle Étoile

Hôtel Esmeralda (£)

Some of the rooms in this old-fashioned yet cosy hotel offer delightful views of Notre-Dame. Beware no lift! Very reasonably priced.

✉ 4 rue St-Julien-le-Pauvre, 75005 ☎ 01 43 54 19 20
🚇 St-Michel

Hôtel Franklin-Roosevelt (£££)

Bright comfortable bedrooms with striking murals and functional bathrooms. You are assured of a warm welcome.

✉ 18 rue Clément Marot, 75008
☎ 01 53 57 49 50;
www.hrooosevelt.com
🚇 Franklin-D Roosevelt

Hôtel du Jeu de Paume (£££)

Exclusive hotel on the Ile Saint-Louis, housed in converted Jeu de Paume (inside tennis court), with striking galleries and mezzanines. Beautiful marble bathrooms.

✉ 54 rue St-Louis-en-l'Ile, 75004 ☎ 01 43 26 14 18;
www.hoteljeudepaume.com
🕐 All year 🚇 Pont-Marie

Hôtel Lenox (££)

The Lenox, in the Saint-Germain district, is elegantly furnished and popular with the design and fashion set. Your breakfast is served in a vaulted cellar.

✉ 9 rue de l'Université 75007
☎ 01 42 96 10 95;
www.lenoxsaintgermain.com
🚇 St-Germain-des-Prés

Hôtel du Lys (£)

Simple hotel at the heart of the Quartier Latin; no lift but modern bathrooms, warm welcome and reasonable prices; book well in advance.

✉ 23 rue Serpente, 75006
☎ 01 43 26 97 57
🚇 St-Michel, Odéon

Hôtel de Nevers (£)

Simple but charming, in a former convent building; private roof terraces for top-floor rooms.

✉ 83 rue du Bac, 75007 ☎ 01 45 44 61 30 🚇 Rue du Bac

Hôtel du Panthéon (££)

An elegant hotel conveniently situated in the university district, with well-appointed air-conditioned bedrooms.

✉ 19 place du Panthéon, 75005
☎ 01 43 54 32 95;
www.hoteldupantheon.com
🚇 Cardinal-Lemoine

Hôtel La Perle (££)

With 38 attractive rooms, this hotel in a renovated 17th-century building is in a quiet street near place St-Sulpice in the Saint-Germain-des-Prés district. Pretty flower courtyard.

✉ **14 rue des Canettes, 75006**
☎ **01 43 29 10 10;**
www.hotellaperle.com
🚇 **Mabillon**

Hôtel Place des Vosges (£)

Picturesque quiet hotel in a 17th-century townhouse, just off the place des Vosges. Lovely views across the rooftops.

✉ **12 rue de Birague, 75004**
☎ **01 42 72 60 46** 🚇 **St-Paul, Bastille**

Hôtel Le Régent (££)

Air conditioning and bright well-appointed bedrooms in this cleverly restored 18th-century house in Saint-Germain-des-Prés.

✉ **61 rue Dauphine, 75006**
☎ **01 46 34 59 80** 🚇 **Odéon**

Hôtel Relais Bosquet (££)

Only a ten-minute walk from the Eiffel Tower and close to Les Invalides, the hotel is spacious and comfortable. You can eat your breakfast overlooking a pretty terrace.

✉ **19 rue du Champ-de-Mars , 75007** ☎ **01 47 05 25 45;**
www.relaisbosquet.com
🚇 **École-Militaire**

Hôtel Relais du Louvre (££)

Warm colours, antique furniture and modern comfort, a stone's throw from the Louvre.

✉ **19 rue des Prêtres St-Germain-l'Auxerrois, 75001**
☎ **01 40 41 96 42;**
www.relaisdulouvre.com
🚇 **Louvre-Rivoli**

Hôtel Ritz Paris (£££)

Sometimes called the palace of kings and the king of palaces, the Ritz shares with the Crillon the top of the list of Paris's luxury hotels. Overlooking the place Vendôme, it boasts a beautiful swimming pool and luxury fitness centre; prices are accordingly very high.

✉ **15 place Vendôme, 75001**
☎ **01 43 16 3070;**
www.ritzparis.com 🚇 **Opéra**

Hôtel Sunny (£)

A welcoming, renovated two star hotel with 37 rooms in the Latin Quarter.

✉ **48 boulevard du Port Royale, 75005** ☎ **01 43 31 79 86;**
www.hotelsunny.com
🚇 **Place Monge**

Hôtel Saint-Honoré (£)

A one-star hotel on the chic rue St-Honoré on the Right Bank. Pristine decor in the 29 rooms. Parking close by.

✉ **85 rue St-Honoré 75001**
☎ **01 42 36 20 38; www.**
hotelsainthonore.com
🚇 **Châlet**

Timhôtel Jardin des Plantes (£)

Attractive 33-roomed hotel in the Latin Quarter opposite the botanical gardens and the Natural History Museum.

✉ **5 rue Linné, 75005** ☎ **01 47 07 06 20; www. timhotel.com**
🚇 **Jussieu**

Timhôtel Montmartre (££)

In the old part of Montmartre, halfway up the hill, with lovely views; attention to detail makes it a comfortable if simple place to stay.

✉ **11 rue Ravignan, 75018**
☎ **01 42 55 74 79; www. timhotel.com** 🚇 **Abbesses**

Budget Hotels and Youth Hostels

Gone are the heady days when Paris was peppered with atmospheric one-star hotels with their inimitable signs '*eau à tous les étages*' (water on every floor). Now there are bath or shower rooms with every bedroom, and correspondingly higher prices and smaller rooms. So don't expect much space in budget hotel rooms, but do expect breakfast and receptionists who speak a second language in every hotel with two or more stars. One way of seeing Paris on a budget is to stay in a youth hostel. Try the Auberge Internationale (✉ 10 rue Trousseau 75011 ☎ 01 47 00 62 00; www.aijparis.com), which offers shared rooms in the heart of the lively Bastille area at rock-bottom prices. Don't expect anything fancy, but the atmosphere is friendly.

101

Disneyland® Park

Shops Galore

'Merchandising' is all part of the entertainment at Disneyland® Resort Paris, and you will find shops everywhere: in the hotels, at Disney® Village, and throughout both of the Disney Parks. It is obviously a highly profitable operation for the Disney organisation, and the commercial tone may displease some visitors. But how much time and money you want to spend shopping is entirely up to you. Just look if you like, and move on.

Tips

Beware of spending too much time in the shops. You will regret not going on the rides if you run out of time, and there are plenty of shops outside the Park to browse in at leisure.

Don't leave things to the last minute when queues are long; shop in the early or mid-afternoon. You can always leave your purchases at the shop and then pick them up from 5PM at Town Square Terrace or have them delivered to your hotel (Disney Hotels and Selected Hotels only).

Besides cash (euros), you can pay for items in Disney shops by traveller's cheque, Eurocheque or credit card, but not by personal cheque. If you are staying in one of the resort's hotels, you can use your Disney Card to charge purchases directly to your credit card account. Currency exchange offices are also available at City Hall, in Adventureland (seasonal) and Fantasyland.

If you buy something faulty, take it back to the shop with your receipt and it will be exchanged. If you have left the Resort, send the item, with a photocopy of the receipt and a letter explaining the defect to the manager of the store where you bought it. Write to him or her c/o Merchandising Department, Disneyland® Paris, BP 100, F-77777 Marne-la-Vallée, CEDEX 4, France. You will then receive a refund or exchange of purchase.

Main Street, U.S.A.

Bixby Brothers Men's Accessories
Situated on Town Square, this elegant shop sells watches, ties, caps, hats, fancy socks and underwear for the man about town.

Boardwalk Candy Palace
No children (and very few adults) get past this in a hurry. Here there are sweets and fudge, chocolates and toffees of all shapes and hues. Glass pillars, jars and a Ferris Wheel are filled with a kaleidoscopic range. Almost behind the scenes, the fudge-makers are hard at work. You can also buy saltwater taffy.

Crystal Art
Yet more Disney souvenirs, in a yesteryear fairground setting. Mickey and Minnie wave from a hot-air balloon. Watch the man making cute little animals out of molten glass at Glass Fantasies.

Dapper Dan's Hair Cuts
A splendid old-style barber's shop with a striped pole outside; inside among the tiles, mahogany and marble are badger-hair brushes and personal shaving mugs. You can have a haircut for about €18, or a haircut and old-fashioned shave for €30.

Disney Clothiers Ltd
Smart fashion gear sold in a draper's shop, set in a lovely house with a fireplace and velvet curtains.

Disney & Co
A multicoloured air balloon with children's clothing, character toys and gifts.

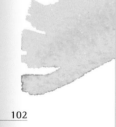

Disneyana Collectibles
Disney collectors should not miss this shop selling ceramics, jewellery boxes, lithographs, and the inked 'cells' from Disney animation pictures. Look for the limited edition books and figurines.

Emporium
Mostly devoted to Disney souvenirs, this is the largest store in the Theme Park. The old-fashioned pneumatic overhead cash transport system is fun to watch.

Harrington's Fine China & Porcelains
The interior of crystal, stained glass and faux marble sets off a glittering array of glass and china. Some hand-painting takes place here.

Lilly's Boutique
Tableware, crystal items, bathrobes and towels, perfumed soap and hand towels all decorated with Disney characters.

Main Street Motors
Souvenirs based on Disney and animated films are sold in a setting with a vintage car theme.

Plaza East and Plaza West Boutiques
Two stands on Central Plaza selling Disney souvenirs, gifts and film.

Ribbons & Bows Hat Shop
Also on Town Square, this shop sells Victorian-style millinery and lots of other things to stick on your head, including hair slides, combs and mouse ears. You can also have a monogram embroidered for free by an old-fashioned sewing machine.

Silhouette Artist
If you fancy your profile sketched, you've come to the right place!

The Storybook Store
Charming little bokshop on Town Square. Disney film classics are retold in many languages – Peter Pan, Alice in Wonderland and so on. Also available are cassettes, novelty stationery, and Tigger is waiting to stamp your books with a Disneyland® Park memento.

Town Square Photography
Film, video cassettes and other photographic equipment is sold in a setting of aged camera gear. There are also repair and express developing services, and cameras and video cameras for hire. Two hour developing service.

Frontierland

Pueblo Trading Post
Interesting range of ethnic Mexican and Indian crafts: rugs, pottery, jewellery, dolls, and more.

Thunder Mesa Mercantile Building
A vast array of Wild West accoutrements, including jeans, coonskin caps, stetsons, cowboy boots and so on, is available at this log cabin. Also Wild-Western-style provisions.

Adventureland

La Bottega di Geppetto
Visit this interesting carver's shop for more unusual toys:

Take Home a Memory
Souvenirs come in all price ranges, from sweets at a few cents to a beautiful glass model of Cinderella's coach at €12,000. Prices of goods at Disneyland® Resort Paris are not low, but then neither is quality, even in items that are mass-produced and basically ephemeral. Whatever you feel about the aesthetics of mouse ears, at least they are not likely to disintegrate the second you walk out of the shop. Disney's rigorous standards apply to every item sold on its property, and that amounts to over 22,000 different pieces of merchandise in more than 40 shops. The shops here are just as much an attraction as the rides.

Shopping Service
All the hotels within Disneyland® Resort Paris provide a shopping service for their guests. Just make your purchases, leave the relevant information and your goods will be delivered direct to your hotel.

music boxes, cuckoo clocks, puzzles, marionettes and baby clothes.

La Boutique de Château
Within the Sleeping Beauty Castle, this festive shop is a year-round hoard of Christmas decorations. Open in summer only.

La Chaumière des Sept Nains
More Disney apparel and stuffed toys, in the cottage of the Seven Dwarfs.

Le Coffre du Capitaine
Pirate gear is on sale in this shop at the exit of Pirates of the Caribbean: pieces-of-eight, cutlasses, eye-patches, skull-and-crossbone hats and flags.

La Confiserie des Trois Fées
Edible goodies in the forest cottage of three good fairies from *Sleeping Beauty*.

La Girafe Curieuse
Set around a buried Land-Rover, under the watchful eye of a giraffe, you will find safari equipment and clothing.

Indiana Jones™ Adventure Outpost
A tantalising collection of odd souvenirs from interesting parts of the globe: jewellery, shells and the necessities of exploration, such as a watch incorporating a compass.

Les Trésors de Schéhérazade
Situated on either side of the entrance to Adventureland, offering sandalwood boxes, brass bells and perfume

bottles, and La Girafe Curieuse (➤ above)

Fantasyland

Merlin l'Enchanteur
Within the castle, this shop is hard to resist. Designed as the magician's workshop, the walls are full of intriguing inventions and glittering toys: figurines, kaleidoscopes, chess sets and even a jewelled crown. Everything your child needs to become a real magician and the costume that goes with it.

La Petite Maison des Jouets
Quaint cottage with a multicoloured roof that offers a wide range of cuddly toys and other sourvenirs.

Sir Mickey's
A fairytale village where Mickey is shown fighting with a giant beanstalk. The two shops here sell Disney momentoes.

Discoveryland

Constellations
Souvenirs for explorers, hi-tech toys and Disney clothes in a startling room rather like a planetarium. An alchemist's still and other scientific instruments decorate the shop. Leonardo's Ornithopter flying machine hangs from the ceiling, with Mickey Mouse at the controls.

Star Traders
All kinds of space-age gadgets and games can be found in this octagonal building: hologram badges, puzzles and so forth.

Elsewhere at
Disneyland® Resort Paris

Walt Disney Studios® Park

Walt Disney Studios Store
The largest boutique in the Park, on Front Lot, offers a variety of toys, clothes and souvenirs, as well as a photo development service.

Studio Photo
Inside the Studio Services precinct on Front Lot, selling cameras, films and souvenirs.

Legends of Hollywood
Located on Front Lot, the striking decor here is straight out of a movie, with an array of souvenirs and gifts from beach gear to toy cars.

Walt Disney Art Classics
This gallery on Animation Courtyard displays a variety of Disney collectibles, including character sketches and cells.

Rock Around the Shop
At the exit of the Rock'n'Roller Coaster ride on Backlot, packed with a choice of music-themed souvenirs.

Disney® Village

The Disney Store
A collection of transport – trains, planes, cars – amid a vast range of 'character merchandise' and clothes for the whole family.

Disney Gallery
Cinema and art lovers will enthuse at the limited series of lithographs and cells on sale here relating to the lastest Disney cartoons. Also china figurines and themed gifts.

Team Mickey
Everything you can imagine in Mickey Mouse sportswear fashion clothing and accessories for adults, children and babies.

Hollywood Pictures
Movie souvenirs (posters, books, photographs and so on), many from the Walt Disney Studios® Park.

Buffalo Trading Company
If you are thinking of setting off for the Wild West, you can get everthing you are likely to need to become a real cowboy here: boots, shirts, hats, bandannas and more.

Rainforest Café Boutique
Souvenir gift shop attached to the Rainforest Café where you can buy a memento of your visit.

World of Toys
Children will be fascinated by the array of unusual toys, games, costumes, jewellery and sweets sold here.

King Ludwig's Castle Store
At the entrance to the castle, this souvenir shop sells King Ludwig merchandise such as T-shirts and beer mugs, as well as themed items – swords, shields, dragons, and lots more.

Hotel Shops
Beside stocking a range of staples, each of the hotel shops features a few special items appropriate to its theme. So Disney's Hotel Cheyenne's® shop sells Wild West gear, and Disney's Hotel Santa Fe's® shop stocks cactus mugs. Do not bother to shop around within the Resort; prices are identical for the same items everywhere.
Images of Mickey Mouse are endlessly reproduced on all manner of artefacts: soft toys, mugs, pencils, T-shirts, sweets and novelties of all kinds. All the hotel shops have significant store space for Disney goods.
The Post Office is in Marne-la-Vallée Station but stamps can also be bought at hotels.

Excursions

Val d'Europe

RER Marne-la-Vallée/Chessy

Val d'Europe International Shopping Centre.
Located next to Disneyland® Resort Paris, this shopping centre was opened in October 2000. Within the complex are some 130 boutique shops and 10 large stores selling everything from fashion and beauty products to home furnishings, gifts and electrical equipment. The hypermarket, Auchan, sells traditional French produce such as cheese and wine.

✉ 14 Cours du Danube, 77711 Marne-la-Vallée

☎ 01 60 42 39 39

La Vallée Outlet Shopping Village
You can find 70 discount outlets offering interna-tional designer brands – fashion and homeware – reducing their prices by at least a third on the previous season's collec-tions. Brands include Polo, Ralph Lauren, Diesel, Burberry, Kenzo and Versace.

✉ 3 Cours de la Garonne, 77700 Serris Marane-la-Vallée

☎ 01 60 42 35 00

Paris

Shopping in Paris is world-renowned with designer boutiques, grandiose department stores, cheap and cheerful chain stores and an array of markets. So with the aid of a good street map to Paris the following are some of the major shopping areas to explore.

Champs Élysées & rue du Faubourg Saint-Honoré
Most top fashion houses are situated in the Champs Élysées area, in particular, avenue Montaigne, avenue Marigny and rue du Faubourg Saint-Honoré. The latter – take the métro to Concorde – is home to all the top names including Prada (No. 6), Hermés (No. 24), Givenchy (No. 28), Jean-Paul Gaultier (No. 30), Yves St Laurent (No. 38), Chloé (No. 54), and Versace (No. 62); you will also find top jewellers such as Cartier (No. 17). Window shopping is a great pastime if you can't afford the high prices. For those on a tighter budget the Champs Élysées is home to a number of high street chain stores and small shopping malls. Close by rue de Royale and place du la Madeleine have some wonderful food shops including the famous foodhall, Fauchon.

Fauchon
✉ 26 place de la Madeleine 75008 ☎ 01 47 42 91 10

Madeleine

Boulevard Haussmann
Take the metro to Chaussée-d'Antin Lafayette and you will emerge on boulevard Haussmann right opposite the stylish department store Galeries Lafayette. The store sells everything except menswear and food, which can be found in the building next door. Down the street is the

store's main competitor, Printemps, made up of three buildings containing women's and children's fashion, homeware and menswear. You can get a great view of Paris from the ninth floor of the Printemps del la Maison building. Chain stores such as Gap and H&M can be found in the streets around the two stores.

Au Printemps
✉ 64 boulevard Haussmann, 75009 Paris
☎ 01 42 82 50 00
Ⓜ Havre-Caumartin

Galeries Lafayette
✉ 40 boulevard Haussmann, 75009 Paris
☎ 01 42 82 34 56
Ⓜ Chaussée d'Antin

Les Marais

This historic area with its narrow streets is home to some of Paris's best small one-off boutiques. This is a great place to wander and you will find plenty of restaurants when the shopping gets too tiring. As well as fashion items there are jewellery shops, home furnishings, designer office accessories, retro shops and second hand clothes shops.

Take the métro to St Paul and have a look at the rue du roi de Sicile for up-to-date clothing and accessories. Other inter-esting streets in Les Marais include rue des Francs-Bourgeois for fashion and rue Vieille-du-Temple, rue Debelleyme and rue St Gilles for those who enthuse over art and antiques.

Saint-Germain-des-Prés

Across the Seine by métro or on foot will bring you to the district of Saint-Germain-des-Prés on the Left Bank. The streets to the south and west of the métro station of Saint. Germain now house smarter designer shops in addition to the more bohemian boutiques usually associated with this area.

In rue Bonaparte you will find names such as Louis Vitton, Emporio Armani and Max Mara and in the rue St Sulpice more boutiques and smart shoe shops. In the rue de Sèvres is Paris's oldest department store Le Bon Marché Rive Gauche famous for its Grande Epicerie, selling specialities from various countries and freshly prepared delicacies, as well as designer clothes, household linens and haberdashery. In the rue de Grenelle are more shoe shops and designer labels as well as shops with classy furniture and fragrant perfume.

Bon Marché Rive Gauche
✉ 24 rue de Sèvres, 75007 Paris
☎ 01 44 39 80 00
Ⓜ Sèvres-Babylone

Carré 'Rive Gauche'

The 'square' formed along the Left Bank by the quai Voltaire, rue de l'Université, rue du Bac and rue des Saints-Pères, which also incorporates the rue de Verneuil, rue de Lille and rue de Beaune, is famous for its concentration of antique dealers.

Street Markets

It is a tradition in France to buy food, and in particular fresh vegetables and fruit, from a market stall, and Paris is no exception. Each *arrondissement* has its covered market, but open-air ones are much more colourful and lively and their higgledy-piggledy displays are definitely more picturesque. To get the feel of these typical Parisian attractions, go to the rue Mouffetard (Ⓜ Monge), the rue de Buci (Ⓜ Odéon) and the rue Lepic (Ⓜ Abbesses). They are open daily except on Mondays. If you are interested in the flea markets, Marché aux Puces de Saint-Ouen is the largest in Paris. Found between Porte de Saint-Ouen and Porte de Cignancourt (Ⓜ Clignancourt) it is open from 9.30–6 on Saturday, Sunday and Monday. Although it is a bit off the beaten track, in the north of the city, you will find a fascinating cross-section of Parisian society and an amazing array of goods for sale. It is still considered the *crème de la crème* of Paris's flea markets.

107

Nightlife & Entertainment

Never a Dull Moment

While the Disney Parks are open Disneyland® Resort Paris is one long round of entertainment. Besides all the individual attractions, there is always something extra going on somewhere. Not all these entertainers are in Disneyland® Park every day. Ask at City Hall if you want to see anything in particular.

Within Walt Disney Studios® Park, back-to-back performances by actors, musicians and characters help to set the scene of a real working film studio. Ask at Studio Services for details of where to catch the acts.

Shows

Performances take place several times a day, at Le Théâtre du Château (featuring Winnie The Pooh and Friends, Too! May–Sep), Videopolis (featuring The Legend of the Lion King), Fantasy Festival Stage or the Chaparral Theatre (featuring the Tarzan™ Encounter May–Sep). Be sure to pick up an Entertainment Program listing show times. The programme rotates weekly, and most shows last about 20 minutes. The Fantasy Festival Stage hosts performances of music and dancing as well as special events such as Christmas shows like Mickey's Winter Wonderland.

Parades and Fireworks

Disney parades and fireworks are an unforgettable part of your Disney experience. The best include, at Disneyland® Park, the Princess Parade – a fanfare of Disney princes and princesses; Disney's Fantillusion Parade, and at Walt Disney Studios®, the Disney Cinema Parade, which takes you behind the scenes of cinema and Disney classics. Tinker Bell's Fantasy in the Sky is the most spectacular display of fireworks high above Sleeping Beauty's Castle (early Jul–3nd Aug). For further details ▶ 33–34).

Dinner Shows

At present there are two dinner shows, one in Disneyland® Park's Frontierland (at The Lucky Nugget Saloon), the other at Disney® Village. The Lucky Nugget Saloon, all gilded lights and tasselled curtains, is horseshoe-shaped like a theatre, and puts on several 30-minute shows a day. The plot is the corny but enjoyable tale of a fun-loving gal who strikes it rich and heads for Paris, where she encounters Pierre Paradis, the man of her dreams, and collects a dance troupe. Buffalo Bill's Wild West Show is more expensive, involving stunt riding, lasso tricks and some bewildered buffalo. It is an enthusiastically presented show featuring 'Annie Oakley' (best of the riders), and assorted cowboys and Indians. Based on the touring Wild West Show which wowed France in the 1889 Exposition Universelle, the theme continues to fascinate its European audience. Western-style spare ribs and chilli accompany the show. There is lots of opportunity for audience participation

Disney® Village

When the Disney Parks close, there are still things to do. In Disney® Village there is a nightclubs and bars, shops and restaurants that all stay open late, as well as multi-screen cinemas (including one with a giant screen) that show English films on selected dates. Hurricanes is the venue for dancing, with 'high-energy' lighting and music, and sunset parties on the veranda (free admission for Disney Hotel guests). Billy Bob's Country Western Saloon has Western music and a Texan atmosphere. Also various live concerts take place on certain dates throughout the year.

Hotel Entertainment

Following the development of night entertainment in Disney® Village, only a stone's throw from most hotels, hotel entertainment is very low-key these days. However, Disney's Davy Crockett Ranch® and Disney's Hotel Cheyenne® continue to provide live country music and karaoke evenings on a regular basis.

Paris

Among the bright lights of Paris any number of high- or low-brow entertainments or restaurants await visitors, from the fleshpots of Pigalle and the Moulin Rouge to the Opéra, or Left-Bank café-théâtre. In addition to the glamorous cabarets, there are world-class ballet, concert and opera venues, scores of nightclubs, café-theatres and atmospheric bars with live music. Also numerous classical music conerts are held in churches. The tourist office outside Marne-la-Vallée will give you lots of advice. Get one of the 'What's On' magazines, such as *L'Officiel des Spectacles* or *Pariscope* (out each Wednesday) for full listings. On Thursdays the Musée d'Orsay, one of Paris's most enjoyable museums, stays open late; and on Mondays or Wednesdays you can visit sections of the Louvre until 10PM. After dark, Paris looks stunning from the top of the Eiffel Tower (open until 11PM), and the *bateaux mouches* run during the evenings, too. Remember to check the time of your last train (usually at about 12:30AM) back to Marne-la-Vallée!

Crazy Horse Saloon

One of the best shows in Paris with beautiful girls and striking colours and lights.

✉ **12 avenue George V, 75008**
☎ **01 47 23 32 32** Ⓜ **Alma-Marceau**

Le Lido

The famous show put on by the Bluebell girls is mostly aimed at tourists but it is still entertaining. It is possible to have dinner on a *bateau-mouche* followed by a show at the Lido.

✉ **116 bis avenue des Champs-Elysées, 75008** ☎ **01 40 76 56 10** Ⓜ **George V**

Moulin-Rouge

Undoubtedly the most famous of them all; its been going since 1889! The show still includes impressive displays of French cancan with stunning costumes and sumptous stage settings.

✉ **82 boulevard de Clichy, 75018**
☎ **01 53 09 82 82** Ⓜ **Blanche**

Opéra Bastille

Paris's 'people's' opera house with its five moveable stages is a technological feat in itself. Opera, recitals, dance and even theatre.

✉ **120 rue de Lyon, 750012**
☎ **08 82 89 90 90** Ⓜ **Bastille**

Other Options

In an attempt not to be outshone in the contest for tourist revenue are several historic towns near Disneyland® Resort Paris. They put on *son et lumière* shows and other events during the summer (Meaux, Fontainebleau and Chantilly). And you can also visit Vaux-le-Vicomte by candlelight on some summer Saturday evenings.

So Much Choice

Paris has a huge number of wonderful bars to choose from. These range from bars selling just beer, to wine, cocktail and late-night bars dotted throughout the city. Most Parisian wine bars are small, neighbourly places, some selling food as well. You will find a great selection of regional wines.

The Paris clubbing is both serious and fickle – serious because no truly cool Parisian turns up before midnight, and fickle because mass loyalties change rapidly. Most clubs keep going through to dawn on Friday and Saturday nights, and nearly all charge for entry (this usually includes a drink).

Sport

More Fun

Additional leisure facilities are available at Disneyland® Resort Paris to cater for the hours of relaxation but facilities are only for guests staying on-site (that is, in appropriate Disney accommodation). All the hotels and Disney® Village have games rooms with a variety of video simulator games and other activities. Children's playgrounds are available at several of the hotels and at Disney's Davy Crockett Ranch®.

Boating

The excitingly landscaped watercourses of Frontierland, the Rivers of the Far West, which run around that interesting piece of Arizona called Big Thunder Mountain, provide Disneyland® Resort Paris guests with an opportunity to take a break from the excitement of the Disney Parks' attractions and to cool down on a hot, sunny day. You can traverse these waters in various craft: River Rogue Keelboats, or two Mississippi-style Paddlewheel Riverboats. These rides, of course, are free once you are inside Disneyland® Park, but they are popular and you may have a long wait for them on days when the Park is crowded.

Cycling

At Disney's Davy Crockett Ranch® bicycles are available for hire by guests staying at the ranch only.

Golf
Golf Disneyland®

Disney's Davy Crockett Ranch® is conveniently close to the golf course, and it is open to the public. Golf Disneyland® is a championship course designed to host top tournaments, but less ambitious golfers of all abilities are welcome to test their skills. Lakes, hills, waterfalls, rocks and the most Disneyish bunkers have been magically bulldozed from flat arable fields, creating a series of varied landscapes that will eventually be sheltered by lush vegetation. Each of the three nine-hole sections of the course is rated par 36, with lengths ranging from 6,781 yards (6,221m) for the championship course to 5,513 yards (5,058m) for the junior course. All facilities are provided: electric golf carts, a driving range, golf-bag storage and a putting green (in the shape of Mickey Mouse's head). The 19th hole has been provided (of course) at the circular Clubhouse Grill, whose windows overlook the putting green. Inside are showers, lockers, a bar and restaurant, and television room. Coaching, a repair and rental service, and a shop selling golfing equipment are also on-site. You can test all aspects of your game in the training area. Group and package rates, and less expensive 'twilight' green fees, are also available. The course is open every day from 8am (or 9am, depending on the season) untill sunset.

Football
Manchester United Soccer School

In April 2004 Disneyland® Resort Paris opened its soccer school, dedicated to one of the world's greatest football clubs. Located opposite Disney's Sequoia Lodge® Hotel, the training camp offers children between the ages of 7 and 14 the opportunity to develop their ball skills through a coaching program developed by Manchester United's Youth Academy. There are three sessions throughout the day (check for times when booking).
☎ 0870 606 6800 (from UK)

Health Clubs

The four more up-market hotels (Disneyland® Hotel, Disney's Hotel New York®, Disney's Newport Bay Club® and Disney's Sequoia Lodge®) have health clubs with gyms, saunas, solariums, massage, steam rooms, Jacuzzis, and so on. They are free to hotel guests, but a charge is payable for the solarium and massage.

Ice-skating

That colourful ornamental pond outside Disney's Hotel New York® freezes over during the winter months and members of the public can use it during three daily sesssions. It costs around €915 per session (€7.62 if you bring your own skates); €6.10 and €4.57 respectively for under-12s.

Jogging

There are two jogging trails, one around Lake Disney®, and one winding through the forest in Disney's Davy Crockett Ranch®. They are for use by resort hotel and campsite guests only.

Swimming Pools

If you are staying in Disney accommodation, one thing you should definitely bring is swimming gear. The four more upmarket hotels, plus Disney's Davy Crockett Ranch®, have their own heated pools. The indoor pools are large and all are imaginatively designed – perhaps the most interesting being the one at the wildness retreat and the pool at Disney's Sequoia Lodge®, with its rocky waterfalls and woodland scenery.

Disneyland® Resort Paris guests should only use the facilities available where they are staying.

Tennis

There are four hard outdoor courts at Disneyland® Resort Paris: two at Disney's Davy Crockett Ranch® and two at Disney's Hotel New York® (the ones at Hotel New York® are floodlit at night and may be used by other Disney hotel guests). There is a charge for use of the courts and reservations must be made. Racquets and balls can be hired on site, but do remember to pack suitable clothes and shoes.

Other Options

If you are staying off-site (not in Disney accommodation), or fancy a whole day of sports activities, you can visit an outdoor leisure centre at Jablines, which can be reached from the N3 (exit at Claye Souilly). Visitors have access to lake swimming (sand beach), riding, tennis, archery, mini-golf, sailing, windsurfing and so on. A single modest entrance charge admits you to the centre; activities are extra. Groups can stay overnight; there is also a campsite. For information about Jablines, ask at the tourist office outside Marne-la-Vallée Station.

If horse-racing is your passion, don't miss the harness-racing at Vicennes with its brilliant flashes of colour-coordinated horses and jockeys. Check the publication *Paris-Turf* for race programmes.

Armchair Sport

If you prefer to be a spectator, try out the Sports Bar in Disney® Village, where numerous TV sets show an endless round of sports programmes. Non-stop sports channels are available on Disneyland® Resort Paris's hotel television network, too.

111

Special Events

Especially for the Children
The parades and shows, and appearances by Disney characters in costume, are the things children seem to love the most. Make sure you have some film in your camera when Mickey Mouse turns up, or you will never be forgiven. You can find Disney characters in Disneyland® Park and Walt Disney® Studios® every day, or at Character Meetings at Café Mickey.

Disneyland Resort Paris
Besides the big parades that take place daily, or whenever Disneyland® Park is open late, special holidays are marked by extra-spectacular extravaganzas. New Year, for example, witnesses even more fireworks than usual and parties in all the hotels. Special parades are held periodically throughout the year. Needless to say, Christmas is celebrated with carols and a tree. Other events are planned at shorter notice during the year.

Paris
January/February
Chinese New Year: In Chinatown.

April/May
International Paris Fair: Gastronomy, homes and gardens and much more at Porte de Versailles.

May
Labour Day (1 May): Processions and symbolic lily-of-the-valley bouquets.

June
Festival Foire Saint-Germain: Village traditions revived.
Fête de la Musique (21 June): Everything from classical to techno, both indoors and out.

July
Bastille Day (14 Jul): The most important French festival is celebrated with fireworks and street dances on the evening of the 13th and a parade on the 14th on the Champs-Élysée.

July–August
Paris, Quartier d'Eté: Open-air music, plays and dance.

Fête des Tuileries: Jardin des Tuileries becomes a fairground (begins end of June).

September
Festival d'Automne à Paris O(mid Sep–end Dec): Music, theatre and dance throughout the city.

October
Faire Internationale d'Art Contemporain: Paris's biggest modern art fair, at the Pavillon du Parc, Paris Expo, Porte de Versailles.
Mondial de l'Automobile: International motor-car show every two years (even years).

November
Beaujolais Nouveau (third Thu in Nov): Copious amounts of wine are drunk when the first bottles hit Paris.

December
Salon nautique international: International boat show at the Porte de Versailles.

Other Options
Several other places within easy reach of Disneyland® Resort Paris have special events, too. In Meaux, for example, there is a summer festival with *son et lumière* in the grounds of the Bishop's Palace. Reims, too, has its viticultural calendar when champagne grapes are harvested. At Fontainebleau surprised visitors may discover a party of Belle Époque Parisians in splendid costumes strolling through the gardens, while Vaux-le-Vicomte offers tours by candlelight on some Saturday nights. The tourist office outside Marne-la-Vallée Station can provide details.

© Disney

Practical Matters

Above: *be sure to get your Fastpass®*

TIME DIFFERENCES

GMT 12 noon	→ France 1PM	→ Germany 1PM	← USA (NY) 7AM	→ Netherlands 1PM	→ Spain 1PM

BEFORE YOU GO

WHAT YOU NEED

● Required
○ Suggested
▲ Not required

Some countries require a passport to remain valid for a minimum period (usually at least six months) beyond the date of entry – contact their consulate or embassy or your travel agent for details.

	UK	Germany	USA	Netherlands	Spain
Passport/National Identity Card	●	●	●	●	●
Visa (Regulations can change – check before your journey)	▲	▲	▲	▲	▲
Onward or Return Ticket	▲	▲	▲	▲	▲
Health Inoculations	▲	▲	▲	▲	▲
Health Documentation (➤ 112, Health)	●	●	●	●	●
Travel Insurance	○	○	○	○	○
Driving Licence (national)	●	●	●	●	●
Car Insurance Certificate (if own car)	●	●	●	●	●
Car Registration Document (if own car)	●	●	●	●	●

WHEN TO GO

Disneyland® Resort Paris

High season

Low season

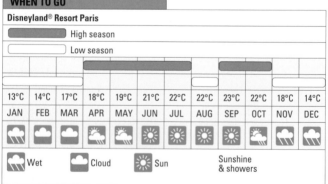

13°C	14°C	17°C	18°C	19°C	21°C	22°C	22°C	23°C	22°C	18°C	14°C
JAN	FEB	MAR	APR	MAY	JUN	JUL	AUG	SEP	OCT	NOV	DEC

🌧 Wet   ☁ Cloud   ☀ Sun   Sunshine & showers

TOURIST OFFICES

In the UK
French Tourist Office,
178 Piccadilly,
London W1J 9AL
☎ 09068 244123
Fax: (020) 7493 6594

In the USA
French Government
Tourist Office,
444 Madison Avenue,
16th floor,
New York NY10022
☎ 410/286 8310
Fax: 212/838 7855

French Government
Tourist Office,
9454 Wilshire Boulevard,
Suite 715,
Beverly Hills CA90212
☎ 310/271 6665
Fax: 310/276 2835

WHEN YOU ARE THERE

WEATHER IN THE AREA

Marne-la-Vallée's climate, described as 'temperate' in Disney's promotional literature, is actually rather drier than that of coastal France. The wettest months are from November to January and from March to May (all have more than 15 days of rainfall – not necessarily, of course, all day long). Highest temperatures are predictably in July and August, when a sunhat is definitely advisable. Between May and June and September and October there are pleasantly equable temperatures, and daytime highs are between 16°C and 21°C (61°C and 70°F). Otherwise, it is unusual to experience climatic extremes or sharp seasonal variations. Average temperatures stay above freezing all year round, and it rarely gets too hot to stay outside in the middle of the day.

DATES TO AVOID

If you have children you may be tied to school holiday times, but to avoid crowds, try to miss popular French holidays, such as Labour Day (Fête du Travail, 1 May), Victory Day (Fête de la Libération, 8 May), Bastille Day (Fête Nationale, 14 July), Assumption (Assomption, 15 August), Hallowe'en/All Saints' (Toussaint, 31 October–1 November), and, of course, Christmas and New Year. You can also expect more crowds around Easter and Whitsuntide. French school holidays are staggered, lasting over several weeks (mid-April to mid-May; early July to early September). August is a traditional holiday month for many Parisians, and those who have not headed for the south coast may well visit the Disneyland® Resort Paris then.

RESERVATIONS

To reserve accommodation or to hire cars at Disneyland® Resort Paris, just call Reservations on 08705 03 03 03 (national rate call), seven days a week. From Ireland, dial 00 44 8705 03 03 03 (international rate call) from Monday to Friday 8AM– 8PM, Saturday 9AM– 6PM (5PM on Sunday). You can also visit the Disneyland® Resort Paris website: http://www.disneylandparis.co.uk or www.disneylandparis.com for information only. From France call 01 60 30 60 30.

TIME

France is on Central European Time (GMT+1). From late March, when clocks are put forward one hour, until late October, French summer time (GMT+2) operates.

CUSTOMS

 YES

From another EU country for personal use (guidelines): 800 cigarettes, 200 cigars, 1kg tobacco, 10 litres of spirits (over 22%), 20 litres of aperitifs, 90 litres of wine, of which 60 litres can be sparkling wine, 110 litres of beer.

From a non-EU country for personal use, the allowances are: 200 cigarettes OR 50 cigars OR 250kg tobacco, 1 litre spirits (over 22%), 2 litres jof intermediary products (e.g. sherry) and sparkling wine, 2 litres of still, wine, 50g perfume, 0.25 litres of eau de toilette. The value limit for goods is €175.

Travellers under 17 years of age are not entitled to the tobacco and alcohol allowances.

 NO

Drugs, firearms, ammunition, offensive weapons, obscene material, unlicensed animals.

EMBASSIES

UK
☎ 01 44 51 31 00

Germany
☎ 01 53 83 45 00

USA
☎ 01 43 12 22 22

Netherlands
☎ 01 40 62 33 00

Spain
☎ 01 44 43 18 00

WHEN YOU ARE THERE

ARRIVING BY AIR

Paris has two main airports, Roissy-Charles-de-Gaulle (01 48 62 22 80), where most international flights arrive, and Orly (01 49 75 15 15). Eurostar trains, direct from London to Paris (☎ 0870 5186 in Britain, ☎ 08 92 35 35 39 in France), take 3 hours.

Roissy/Charles-de-Gaulle Airport
Kilometres to city centre   **Journey times**

23 kilometres

	45 minutes
	50 minutes
	30–60 minutes

Orly Airport
Kilometres to city centre   **Journey times**

14 kilometres

	40 minutes
	30 minutes
	20–40 minutes

Both airports are served by shuttle buses (*navettes*) which depart for Disneyland® Resort Paris every 20 minutes at peak times, every hour at other times. Journey times vary according to traffic density. Buses cost the same from either airport (adult €14, child €11.50; transfer fares are included in Disney hotel packages). Passengers are taken to each of the Disneyland® Resort Paris hotels in turn, or dropped at the bus station, very near the entrance of the Disney Parks. If you are staying at Disney's Davy Crockett Ranch®, you will have to get a taxi from the station to the ranch.

 Internal Flights Air France is the leading domestic airline in France. For flight information ☎ 08 20 82 08 20. Daily departures from Orly and Roissy/Charles-de-Gaulle airports connect Paris with most major French cities and towns in an average flight time of one hour.

ARRIVING BY CAR

Disneyland® Resort Paris lies about 20 miles (32km) due east of Paris, off exit 14 of the A4 (Autoroute de l'Est, leading to Germany, Austria and Luxembourg) Nancy–Metz motorway (the route to Strasbourg) in the sprawling area of Marne-la-Vallée, *département* Seine-et-Marne. If you approach from another direction, to avoid the capital, you will probably use the Francilienne (A104 and N104), linking motorways A1 (Autoroute du Nord, bound for the Channel ports, UK and Low Countries), A4, A6 (Autoroute du Soleil, heading south for the Riviera, Italy and Switzerland), and A10 (L'Aquitaine, which goes via Bordeaux towards Spain and Portugal). Follow signs to Marne-la-Vallée (Val d'Europe) until you see signposts for the Resort. French motorways are toll roads, but they are free in the Paris area.
Leave the motorway at exit 14 and follow signs for Disneyland® Resort Paris. If you are staying at a Disney hotel you can use the hotel car park; if not, park in the main lot (€8 per day – 2004 prices). The car park is huge (space for over 9,000 vehicles), so note carefully where you leave your car. Each sector is named after a Disney character. Moving walkways speed up the journey from the car park to the main entrances. Cars cannot be left overnight in the car park. If you have engine trouble, or forget where you left your car, ask cast members for help.

WHEN YOU ARE THERE

ARRIVING BY RAIL

The Parisian suburban railway (RER) now extends as far as Disneyland® Resort Paris. The station is Marne-la-Vallée–Chessy, about two minutes' walk from the entrances of both Disney Parks. Journey time is about 40 minutes from central Paris (Châtelet–les–Halles Métro link), but you need to be careful which train you take. It is a branched line (take Line A4, not Line A2 for Boissy–St-Léger), and not all the trains continue as far as Marne-la-Vallée. Check the platform indicators before you board, and make sure the correct light is showing. The single fare is €6. Trains run until about midnight. The high-speed TGV train now stops at Marne-la-Vallée–Chessy Station, putting Disneyland® Resort Paris just 1 hour 48 minutes from Lyon, 63 minutes from Lille and only 3 hours from London's Waterloo Station via the Euro Tunnel.

MONEY

The euro is the official currency of France. Euro banknotes and coins were introduced in January 2002. Banknotes are in denominations of 5, 10, 20, 50, 100, 200 and 500 euros and coins are in denominations of 1, 2, 5, 10, 20 and 50 cents, and 1 and 2 euros. Euro traveller's cheques are widely accepted, as are major credit cards. Credit and debit cards can also be used for withdrawing euro notes from cashpoint machines. Cashpoints are widely accessible throughout the city. France's former currency, the French franc, went out of circulation in early 2002.

EXCHANGE

Exchange facilities can be found at the Main Entrances of the Disney Parks, and in the two information booths in Adventureland and Fantasyland. You can also change money in Disney® Village, and at any accommodation reception desk (if you are a resident). The rates given are standard throughout the Resort. They are on the low side, but service is pleasant and efficient, and no commission is charged. You may get a slightly better commission-free rate in central Paris if you happen to be there, but it is not worth making a special journey. Remember that you will need your passport if you want to change traveller's cheques.

ATMs are available in the two arcades in Main Street, U.S.A., in Discoveryland, Adventureland, next to Studio Services and at the Backlot Express Restaurant.

All shops and hotels, most restaurants and the campsite will accept major credit cards (American Express, Visa, Eurocard/Mastercard); personal or traveller's cheques drawn in euros (with valid ID), Eurocheques or banknotes (euros). Disneyland® Resort Paris hotel guests may charge items to their hotel accounts using a special card which they receive as they check in.

CENTIMETRES

INCHES

WHEN YOU ARE THERE

TOURIST OFFICES

Disneyland Resort Paris
Seine-et-Marne and Île-de-France tourist office is situated outside Marne-la-Vallee–Chessy Station and is a very good source of information and leaflets on local sights, hotels and restaurants. There is also a video and laser presentation. It is well worth a visit (tel: 01 60 43 33 33).

● place des Passagers-du-Vent, Marne-la-Vallée, 77705
☎ 01 60 43 33 33
🚇 RER line A, Marne-la-Vallée–Parc Disneyland

Paris
● Office de Tourisme de Paris
(Paris Tourism Bureau), 25 rue des Pyramides, 75001 Paris
☎ 08 92 68 30 10
www.paris-touristoffice.com
🚇 Daily 9AM–8PM (Sun/pub hols, Nov–Mar, 11AM–7PM)

Branches
● Gare de Lyon
🕐 Mon–Sat 8AM–6PM

● Tour Eiffel (Eiffel Tower)
🕐 May–Sep: daily 11AM–6:40PM

Paris Île-de-France
● Carrousel du Louvre (lower level)
☎ 01 44 50 19 98/ 0826 16 66 66
www.Paris-ile-de-france.com
🕐 Daily 10AM

FRENCH NATIONAL HOLIDAYS

J	F	M	A	M	J	J	A	S	O	N	D
1		(1)	(1)	3(4)	(1)	1	1			2	1

1 Jan	New Year's Day
Mar/Apr	Easter Sunday and Monday
1 May	Labour Day
8 May	VE Day
May	Ascension Day
May/Jun	Whit Sunday and Monday
14 July	Bastille Day
15 Aug	Assumption Day
1 Nov	All Saints' Day
11 Nov	Remembrance Day
25 Dec	Christmas Day

Banks, businesses, museums and most shops (except boulangeries) are closed on these days in France. NB. this does not apply to Disney Parks

OPENING HOURS IN PARIS

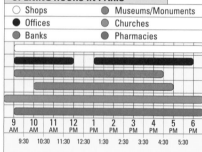

○ Shops ● Museums/Monuments
● Offices ● Churches
● Banks ● Pharmacies

9 AM	10 AM	11 AM	12 PM	1 PM	2 PM	3 PM	4 PM	5 PM	6 PM
	9:30	10:30	11:30	12:30	1:30	2:30	3:30	4:30	5:30

In addition to the times shown above, some shops close between noon and 2PM and all day Sunday and Monday. Large department stores open from 9:30AM to 6:30PM and until 9 or 10PM one or two days a week. Food shops open 7AM to 1:30PM and 4:30 to 8PM; some open Sunday until noon. Some banks are open extended hours, including Saturday morning but most banks close weekends. Museum and monument opening times vary but national museums close Tuesday (except the Musée d'Orsay, Versailles and the Trianon Palace which close Monday), while most other city museums usually close Monday.

PUBLIC TRANSPORT – PARIS

 RER The RER (pronounced 'ehr-oo-ehr') is the fast suburban rail service, which also serves the Paris city centre. There are five lines (*lignes*): A, B, C, D and E, and it is connected with the métro and SNCF suburban network. Services run 5:30AM to midnight, with trains every 12 minutes.

 Métro Paris's underground with over 300 stations ensures you are never more than 500m from a métro stop. Lines are numbered 1 to 14 and are known by the names of the stations at each end. Follow the orange *correspondance* signs to change lines. The métro runs daily 5:30AM to 12:30AM.

 Buses Buses are a good way of seeing Paris (especially route 24), although traffic can be very heavy. Bus stops show the numbers of buses that stop there. Buses run 6:30AM to 8:30PM with a reduced service on Sunday and after 8:30PM. Bus tickets are the same as those for the métro.

CAR RENTAL

 Hertz is the official Disneyland® Resort Paris car-hire company, with a rental office in Marne-la-Vallée–Chessy TGV/RER Station. Guests staying at the Resort receive concessionary rates, which are pretty competitive. If you are based at the Resort and just want a car to tour the area for a few days, this is by far the most convenient way to do it. If you are staying off-site, check out competing rates at various airport offices. You can also book cars through Disneyland® Resort Paris's Central Reservations Office (➤ 115).

TAXIS

Taxis can be hailed if you see one with its roof light on. Taxis are metered with a surcharge for luggage, journeys after 10PM and before 6:30AM, and for going from and to stations and airports. Queues can be long, particularly at railway stations.

DRIVING IN FRANCE

 Speed limits on toll motorways (*autoroutes*) **130kph** (**110kph** when wet). Non-toll motorways and dual carriageways: **110kph** (**100kph** when wet). Paris ring road (*périphérique*): **80kph**

 Speed limits on country roads: **90kph (80kph** when wet)

 Speed limits on urban roads: **50kph**

 Must be worn in front seats at all times and in rear seats where fitted.

 Random breath-testing frequent. Limit: 0.05 per cent alcohol in blood.

 Leaded petrol is sold as *essence super* (98 octane). Unleaded is available in two grades: *essence sans plomb* (95 octane) and *essence super sans plomb* (98 octane). Diesel (*Gasoil* or *Gazole*) is also readily available. In Paris filling stations can be hard to spot, often consisting of little more than a few kerb-side pumps.

 If your car breaks down in France contact the 24-hour repair service (☎ 01 45 31 16 20). On motorways (*autoroutes*) use the orange-coloured emergency phones (located every mile/2km) to contact the breakdown service.

TOILETS

There are lots of these, discreetly placed around the Resort. They are regularly cleaned and serviced and mostly exemplary, though some are a little cramped. What you will find outside the Resort, however, is another matter – and mostly best forgotten.

WHEN YOU ARE THERE

HEALTH

Insurance
Nationals of EU countries can obtain medical treatment at reduced cost in France with the relevant documentation (Form E111 for Britons), although private medical insurance is still advised and is essential for all other visitors.

Medical Treatment
Minor ailments can often be treated by pharmacies (► below, drugs). All public hospitals have a 24-hour emergency service (*urgences*) as well as specialist doctors. Payment is made on the spot but if you are hospitalised ask to see the *assistante sociale* to arrange payment directly through your insurance.

Sun Advice
July and August (when most French people go to the coast) are the sunniest (and hottest) months. If 'doing the sights' cover up or apply a sunscreen and take on plenty of fluids. To escape the sun altogether try an inside attraction.

Drugs
Pharmacies – recognised by their green cross sign – employ highly qualified staff able to offer medical advice, provide first-aid and prescribe a wide range of drugs, though some are available by prescription (*ordonnance*) only.

Safe Water
It is quite safe to drink tap water in France, but never drink from a tap marked *eau non potable* (not drinking water). Many prefer the taste of mineral water, which is fairly cheap and widely available in several brands.

Dental Services
As for general medical treatment (see above, **Insurance**), nationals of EU countries can obtain dental treatment at reduced cost. Around 70 per cent of standard dentists' fees are refunded. Still, private medical insurance is advised for all.

PERSONAL SAFETY

Petty crime, particularly theft of wallets and handbags is fairly common in Paris. Be aware of innocent, scruffy-looking children, they may be working the streets in gangs, fleecing unwary tourists. Report any loss or theft to the *Police Municipale* (blue uniforms). To be safe:
● Watch your bag on the métro, in busy tourist areas like Beaubourg and the Champs-Elysées and in museum queues.

Police assistance:
☎ **17** from any call box

ELECTRICITY

The power supply in France is: 220 volts
Sockets accept two-round-pin (or increasingly three-round-pin) plugs, so an adaptor is needed for most non-Continental appliances and a voltage transformer for appliances operating on 100–120 volts.

ENTRANCE TICKETS

There are two tiers of charges: one for children aged between three and eleven inclusive and one for anyone aged twelve or over. Children under three enter free of charge. In addition, you can buy an Entrance Ticket for one or three days (the extended ticket is cheaper pro rata than the one-day ticket); it does not have to be used on consecutive days but must be used within the three-year validity period. Annual Entrance Tickets are also available, giving unlimited entry for one year. Entrance charges are subject to constant revision (not necessarily upwards, either – Disney is well aware of market forces). Your Entrance Ticket entitles you to unlimited use of any of the attractions, shows and parades within the Theme Park of your choice (one-day ticket) or both Disney Parks (three-day ticket) during operating hours, except the Rustler Roundup Shootin' Gallery in Frontierland and the Video Games Arcade in Discoveryland in the Disneyland® Park.

CHARGES

These prices are intended as a guide, and were current at the time of going to press. Prices should be checked with Disneyland® Resort Paris at the time of your visit. Anyone aged 12 or over counts as an adult and must pay the full entrance price. Children under three can enter free.

1-day Disney Park Entrance Ticket: (high or low-season): Adult €40, Child (3-11) €30
2-day 'Hopper' Ticket: Adult €89, Child €69
3-day 'Hopper' Ticket: Adult €109, Child €84
2-Park Annual Ticket: Adult €229, Child €199
Car parking: €8 per day
Shuttle Buses/Airport Buses: €14 (single adult fare); €11.50 (child fare)
RER from central Paris: €6 (single adult fare); €3 (child)
Animal Care Center: €8 per day (including food), or €12 overnight
Wheelchair or pushchair rental: €6.10 per day (not to be taken outside the Disney Parks)
Buffalo Bill's Wild West Show (Disney Village): Adult €49.50, Child €29.50 (drinks and dinner included).

OPENING TIMES

Disneyland® Resort Paris Disney Parks can be visited 365 days a year. Officially, the Parks open at 9AM most days – 10AM weekdays from September to mid-March – but often they open earlier. Disneyland® Resort Paris guests will find little notes in their bedrooms saying 'Just for you, the Disney Parks open earlier'. Actually, anyone who turns up can get in. During peak seasons, you can usually get inside the gates at least half an hour before the official opening time, though attractions open at the usual time. Weekdays are generally less busy than weekends, and Tuesday is an especially quiet day. On Mondays many shops and other businesses are closed and families often go out together. Schools close on Wednesdays, so this is a popular day with French children. Closing times change according to season, holiday periods, weather conditions and demand. Although the turnstiles may allow no more visitors in if the Disney Parks become too crowded, guests staying in Disneyland® Resort Paris accommodation always have entry. Check what time the Disney Parks close as you enter: in high summer Disneyland® Park often stays open until 11PM. For full details 08705 03 03 03 (from UK). The golf course is open 8AM/9PM until sunset and the Clubhouse Grill stays open until one hour after sunset.

PHOTOGRAPHY

Films, batteries and a developing service are available in any hotel shop and at several shops in the Disney Parks. The specialist photographic equipment store is Town Square Photography in Main Street, U.S.A., where you can buy or rent cameras and video cameras, and have film developed the same day. Studio Photo in Walt Disney Studios® Park (Front Lot) sells cameras and film, and Walt Disney Studios Store offers a photo development service. Look for the 'Point Photo' signs, which show good places for a picture. You are not allowed to take flash photographs, or to use video cameras within attractions.

IN THE DISNEY PARKS

GUIDED TOURS

Guided tours can be booked from City Hall in Town Square and Studio Services in Front Lot. They last between 1 and 2 hours. Special tours can be organised for private groups by arrangement.

CONCESSIONS

Senior Citizens Groups of 25 senior citizens (over 55s) or more qualify for a 20 per cent reduction in Theme Park entrance fees (this offer may not be valid during peak periods). Cast members are always happy to help anyone with special needs. It may be worth getting a Carte Senior, which is valid for all women over 60 and all men over 65, and entitles the bearer to reductions of up to 50 per cent in Paris museums, on public transport and in places of entertainment. The card costs €45 for unlimited travel (2002 price). To get one, simply take your passport to the Abonnement office of any main railway station. The card is valid for a year. If you do not have one, wave your passport when you have to pay and you may still be able to get a discount.

TELEPHONES

Both coin-operated and card phones are available in the Disney Parks, in Disney® Village and in Resort accommodation. France Télécom phone cards are on sale at the post office, in shops, and at the golf course. Telephone charges are the same in all hotels and in the campsite. They include a mark-up over normal France Télécom rates, depending upon what time of day you call.

International Dialling Codes

From France to:

UK: 00 44

POST

Post office
This can be found at Marne-la-Vallée–Chessy Station and is usually open from 9am till 7pm, seven days a week, but not on public holidays. Stamps can be bought at many shops, including The Storybook Store in Town Square, inside Disneyland® Park. Postboxes can be found throughout the Disney Parks, and in the hotels and Disney's Davy Crockett Ranch®.

TIPS/GRATUITIES

As a rule, it is not necessary to leave tips in Disneyland® Resort Paris, however you may feel inclined to leave something in a table-service restaurant, or to tip a member of staff who has been particularly helpful. Outside the Disney Parks check whether service is included (service compris) before you pay the bill. It is customary to leave small change in a saucer at a bar or café. Porters, cinema usherettes, tour guides and Paris's cabbies all expect tips.

IN THE DISNEY PARKS

MEDICAL CENTRES

First-aid centres with fully trained nursing staff are located next to Plaza Gardens Restaurant in Main Street, U.S.A. and behind Studio Services in Front Lot. Simple medical supplies can be found in all the hotels. If there is a serious problem, ask your hotel receptionist or the tourist office for advice. There is a pharmacy in Coupvray, a medical centre in Esbly, and a hospital in Lagny.

SECURITY

Disneyland® Resort Paris makes its own security arrangements, very discreetly but very efficiently. Security staff can be summoned instantly to any trouble spot. Take sensible precautions with your valuables as, with all crowded places, it can be a honeypot for pickpockets and bag snatchers. If you are leaving a vehicle in the car park remember to lock it and to leave belongings where they are out of sight.

VIS!TORS WITH DISABILITIES

Ask for the Disabled Guest Guide at the main entrance, City Hall or at Studio Services. This gives full details of facilities for disabled visitors. The Resort is designed to be as user-friendly as possible for all guests, but wheelchair users will need someone in their party who can lift them out of their chair and on to rides. Special vehicles can be provided to help guests reach the Disney Parks from the hotels and campsite, and all hotels have rooms designed for the disabled. Parking spaces near the entrance are also available. Wheelchairs can be rented in Town Square at Main Street U.S.A or at Studio Services in Front Lot (€6.10 per day; they must not be taken outside the Disney Parks). Priority is given to the disabled for places to see parades and shows. Ask any cast member for advice. All WC blocks, shops and restaurants are accessible by wheelchair, and some shops have special dressing-rooms. If you need assistance, enquire at City Hall, First Aid (near Plaza Gardens Restaurant) or Studio Services. If you have a weak back or neck, avoid the joltier rides such as Big Thunder Mountain, Indiana Jones™ and the Temple of Peril: Backwards, Space Mountain, Star Tours and Rock'n'Roller Coaster starring Aerosmith. Special aids are available for sight-impaired guests.

LOST AND FOUND

Stray children are taken to the Lost Children Office on Central Plaza or at Studio Services, where they are looked after until their guardians turn up. Enquire for them here, at any information booth, at Guest Relations, or at City Hall. Lost or found property should be notified to City Hall in Town Square or Studio Services in Front Lot, where you can also leave a message for separated companions. If you lose anything in your hotel, contact Housekeeping. Safe deposit boxes are provided at all reception areas.

PETS

The only animals allowed within the Resort to compete with Mickey and friends are guide dogs. Near the car park is the Animal Care Center, where trained staff will care for your dog for a charge of €8 per day, including food and exercise (€12 extra overnight – 2002 prices). However, pets are only accepted at the Animal Care Center if owners can produce relevant certificates of health, or proof of vaccination.

WHEN DEPARTING

- Contact the airport or airline on the day prior to leaving to ensure flight details are unchanged.
- It is advisable to arrive at the airport two hours before the flight is due to take off.
- Check the duty-free limits of the country you are entering before departure.

LANGUAGE

You will usually hear well-enunciated French in Paris, spoken quite quickly and in a myriad of accents as many Parisians come from the provinces. English is spoken by those involved in the tourist trade and by many in the centre of Paris – less so in the outskirts. However, attempts to speak French will always be appreciated. Below is a list of a few words that may be helpful. The gender of words is indicated by (m) or (f) for masculine and feminine. More extensive coverage can be found in the AA's *Essential French Phrase Book* which lists over 2,000 phrases and 2,000 words.

hotel	*hôtel (m)*	rate	*tarif (m)*
room	*chambre (f)*	breakfast	*petit déjeuner (m)*
..single/double	*une personne /deux personnes (f)*	toilet	*toilette (f)*
		bathroom	*salle de bain (f)*
...one/two nights	*une/deux nuits (f)*	shower	*douche (f)*
...per person/per room	*par personne/par chambre*	balcony	*balcon (m)*
		key	*clef/clé (f)*
reservation	*réservation (f)*	room service	*service de chambre*
bank	*banque (f)*	English pound	*livre sterling (f)*
exchange office	*bureau de change (m)*	American dollar	*dollar (m)*
		banknote	*billet (m)*
post office	*poste (f)*	coin	*pièce (f)*
cashier	*caissier (m)*	credit card	*carte de crédit (f)*
foreign exchange	*change (m)*	traveller's cheque	*chèque de voyage (m)*
currency	*monnaie (f)*	giro cheque	*chèque postal (m)*
restaurant	*restaurant (m)*	starter	*hors d'oeuvres (m)*
café	*café (m)*	main course	*plat principal (m)*
table	*table (f)*	dish of the day	*plat du jour (m)*
menu	*carte (f)*	dessert	*dessert (m)*
set menu	*menu (m)*	drink	*boisson (f)*
wine list	*carte des vins (f)*	waiter	*garçon (m)*
lunch	*déjeuner (m)*	waitress	*serveuse (f)*
dinner	*dîner (m)*	the bill	*addition (f)*
aeroplane	*avion (m)*	...first/second class	*première/deuxième classe (f)*
airport	*aéroport (m)*		
train	*train (m)*	ticket office	*guichet (m)*
...station	*gare (f)*	timetable	*horaire des départs et des arrivées (m)*
bus	*l'autobus (m)*		
...station	*gare routière (f)*		
ferry	*bateau (m)*	seat	*place (f)*
...port	*port (m)*	non-smoking	*non-fumeurs*
ticket	*billet (m)*	reserved	*réservée*
...single/return	*simple/retour*	taxi!	*taxi! (m)*
yes	*oui*	help!	*au secours!*
no	*non*	today	*aujourd'hui*
please	*s'il vous-plaît*	tomorrow	*demain*
thank you	*merci*	yesterday	*hier*
hello	*bonjour*	how much?	*combien?*
goodbye	*au revoir*	expensive	*cher*
goodnight	*bonsoir*	closed	*fermé*
sorry	*pardon*	open	*ouvert*

INDEX

Acknowledgements
The Automobile Assocation wishes to acknowledge that the main pictures in this book
are © Disney Worldwide.

The remaining photographs are from the Association's own library (**AA WORLD TRAVEL
LIBRARY**) with contributions from the following:
Max Jourdan 71, 72, 73, 75t, 76t, 77t, 78t, 78c, 79, 80, 81, 120; David Noble 75b; 77c;
Bernard Rieger 76b; Tony Souter 70, 82b; Wyn Voysey 82t

Dear Essential Traveller

**Your comments, opinions and recommendations are very
important to us. So please help us to improve our travel
guides by taking a few minutes to complete this simple
questionnaire.**

*You do not need a stamp (unless posted outside the UK). If you do not want to cut this page
from your guide, then photocopy it or write your answers on a plain sheet of paper.*

Send to: **The Editor, AA World Travel Guides,
FREEPOST SCE 4598, Basingstoke RG21 4GY.**

Your recommendations...

We always encourage readers' recommendations for restaurants, nightlife
or shopping – if your recommendation is used in the next edition of the
guide, we will send you a *FREE* AA *Essential* **Guide** of your choice.
Please state below the establishment name, location and your reasons
for recommending it.

_____
_____
_____
_____

Please send me **AA *Essential*** _____

About this guide...

Which title did you buy?
   AA *Essential* _____
Where did you buy it? _____
When? m̲ m̲ / y̲ y̲

Why did you choose an AA *Essential* Guide? _____

_____
_____
_____

Did this guide meet your expectations?
   Exceeded ☐ Met all ☐ Met most ☐ Fell below ☐
   Please give your reasons_____

_____
_____
_____

continued on next page...

Were there any aspects of this guide that you particularly liked? _____

_____

_____

_____

Is there anything we could have done better? _____

_____

_____

_____

_____

About you...

Name (*Mr/Mrs/Ms*) _____

Address _____

_____

_____ Postcode _____

Daytime tel nos _____

Which age group are you in?
Under 25 ☐ 25–34 ☐ 35–44 ☑ 45–54 ☑ 55–64 ☑ 65+ ☐

How many trips do you make a year?
Less than one ☑ One ☑ Two ☐ Three or more ☑

Are you an AA member? Yes ☑ No ☐

About your trip...

When did you book? m m / y y   When did you travel? m m / y y

How long did you stay? _____

Was it for business or leisure? _____

Did you buy any other travel guides for your trip?

If yes, which ones? _____

_____

Thank you for taking the time to complete this questionnaire. Please send
it to us as soon as possible, and remember, you do not need a stamp
(*unless posted outside the UK*).

Happy Holidays!